This is the Henry Holt Walks Series,
which originated with
PARISWALKS *by Alison and Sonia Landes*
Other titles in the series include:

JERUSALEMWALKS *by Nitza Rosovsky*
FLORENCEWALKS *by Anne Holler*
ROMEWALKS *by Anya M. Shetterly*
VIENNAWALKS *by J. Sydney Jones*
VENICEWALKS *by Chas Carner and Alessandro Giannatasio*
RUSSIAWALKS *by David and Valeria Matlock*
BARCELONAWALKS *by George Semler*
BEIJINGWALKS *by Don J. Cohn and Zhang Jingqing*
NEW YORKWALKS *by The 92nd Street Y*
MADRIDWALKS *by George Semler*
BERLINWALKS *by Peter Fritzsche and Karen Hewitt*
PRAGUEWALKS *by Ivana Edwards*

LONDONWALKS

REVISED EDITION

Anton Powell

*Photographs by Robin Laurance
and Leonard Wolff*

An Owl Book

Henry Holt and Company • New York

Henry Holt and Company, Inc.
Publishers since 1866
115 West 18th Street
New York, New York 10011

Henry Holt® is a registered trademark
of Henry Holt and Company, Inc.

Copyright © 1981, 1991 by Anton Powell
Photographs copyright © 1981, 1991 by Robin Laurance and
copyright © 1991 by Leonard Wolff
All rights reserved.
Published in Canada by Fitzhenry & Whiteside Ltd.,
195 Allstate Parkway, Markham, Ontario L3R 4T8.

Library of Congress Cataloging-in-Publication Data
Powell, Anton.
Londonwalks / Anton Powell : photographs by
Robin Laurance
and Leonard Wolff.—Rev. ed.
        p.   cm.
"An Owl book."
Includes index.
1. London (England)—Description—Tours. 2. Walking—
England—London. I. Title.
DA679.P68   1991   90-40012
914.2104'858—dc20   CIP

ISBN 0-8050-1300-8 (An Owl Book: pbk.)

Henry Holt books are available for special promotions
and premiums. For details contact: Director, Special Markets.

Second Edition

Designed by Claire Naylon Vaccaro

Printed in the United States of America
All first editions are printed on acid-free paper.∞

5   7   9   10   8   6   4

To Bernadine McGuire

Contents

Acknowledgments
xi

Introduction
1

Information and Advice
3

First Impressions 3 ▪ Transportation 5 ▪ Hotels 6
Restaurants and Shops 8 ▪ Tipping 9 ▪ Shop-
ping 9 ▪ Pubs 11 ▪ Cinemas 13 ▪ Entertainments 13
Newspapers 13 ▪ Asking for Information 14 ▪ Help 14
Telephones 15 ▪ Glossary 15

Walk 1
The London Dickens Knew:
Adelphi and Covent Garden
21

Walk 2
Legal and Illegal London:
The Inns of Court
75

Walk 3
The Old Palace Quarter:
St. James's
127

Walk 4
London's Latin Quarter:
Chelsea
173

Walk 5
The Backstairs of Government:
Westminster and Whitehall
215

Restaurants, Pubs, and Shops
246

Index
251

Acknowledgments

Although there were many people who helped me, there is space to mention only a few. Dr. Sarah Potter read the whole of my manuscript patiently, promptly, and with a scholarly eye. Jane Fallis contributed important improvements to its style. Alan Myers gave professional help on points of law, and Dr. David Tucker advised on the subject of Dickens. Pam Wierengo and Madge Caro put their wide knowledge of Chelsea at my disposal. Tony Sympson told me about the history of Goodwin's Court, the seventeenth-century street he and his family have preserved. Holly Brennan gave efficient and courteous help in the Chelsea Public Library. Leonard Wolff acted with speed and generosity as photographer for Walk 5.

Almost every writer on London's history is, or ought to be, deeply indebted to the many-volumed *Survey of London*, long published by the Greater London Council. After inspecting the often fanciful works of local historians, I found it a frequent pleasure and relief to turn to the *Survey*, with its meticulous attention to sources. Also valuable were Thea Holme's *Chelsea* and Kellow Chesney's magnificent book *The Victorian Underworld*—a factual guide to the seedy glamour of Dickens's London.

Susan Poate first made London for me a magical city.

WALKS AND MAIN SIGHTS

Central London

Walk 1: Adelphi and Covent Garden
Walk 2: The Inns of Court
Walk 3: St. James's
Walk 4: Chelsea
Walk 5: Westminster and Whitehall

Introduction

This book aims to show you places that visitors rarely find, and which British people themselves often know little about. Most of London is still undiscovered. There are pubs gleaming with Victorian mahogany and etched glass that have no signs to inform you of their age. In Covent Garden, one of the areas we shall visit, whole streets are still lit by nineteenth-century gaslights, yet no one pays them much attention—the local people don't notice because the lights are perfectly efficient (that is why they're still there); and visitors usually don't see them because much of Covent Garden, like most of the districts we shall look at, is off the well-traveled tourist routes.

I've tried to make this book a "good read" for home or hotel, and also an accurate guide on the ground. It contains five walks, each taking about 2½ hours, a pace which allows you to look at places in proper detail—at metal cones by house doors used for putting out torches in the eighteenth century, at tiny windows barred against nineteenth-century child thieves, at forgotten courtyards and at specialty, sometimes eccentric, businesses.

London has to be discovered on foot. Trying to learn about it from a tourist bus or a car would be rather like trying to learn about the United States from a plane. The views would be interesting and often magnificent, but it would be hard to find out much about the people and their history.

Guidebooks, even some of the best, can be superficial if they try to cover huge areas of the city. Here is an example:

> The narrow St. James's Place, opening on the west here, has a variety of pleasant old houses. Spencer House, on the left facing Green Park, is a large mansion in a classical style built in 1765 by John Vardy and restored in 1957 after war damage. No. 26, next to it, is a distinctive block of flats [apartments] by Denys Lasdun (1959).

Just three sentences for a fascinating seventeenth-century street that we shall be visiting. It was the street where, in the 1660s, a powerful royal mistress had an elaborate underground "freezer" for wine; where, in the 1820s, the artist who did the original and outrageous "Tom and Jerry" cartoons lived; and where you can also see the splendid, gaslit home of a famous politician who came to a tragic end in 1830. A street like this needs, and will get, pages to itself.

To help you find the places along the walks, I have often used measurement in yards ("Ten yards farther, on the left . . ."). By a yard I mean just a longish stride. I hope this method is less frustrating than the more traditional guidebook vocabulary of "nearby" and "farther down the street." After a while you will know whether my paces are shorter or longer than yours, and you can make the necessary adjustments.

Information
and Advice

FIRST IMPRESSIONS

In almost any foreign country some things are better, some worse, than at home. On the first days of a vacation it's easy to be either starry-eyed or unreasonably depressed. But you will soon notice trade-offs. In England, pubs, theaters, and public transport are a big plus; restaurants less so. The public discipline of the British in forming queues (lines) on the pavement (sidewalk) is often admired, but their indiscipline on the roads is sometimes frightening. You will find, too, that the British think *they* are the ones who speak English—there's an old line about England and America being divided by a common language—even though Americans often come closer to reproducing the English of Shakespeare's day. There is a selected glossary of differences between the American and British dialects later in this chapter. Young people's slang in Britain is largely American in origin, but you may find older people's slang less familiar. For instance, to the young the police are often "fuzz" and sometimes even

"Feds," even though Britain has no FBI and is not a federation. For older folk the police can be "rozzers" or "Old Bill." The word *bobbies* is now genteel, dated, and rarely used.

British dress differs slightly from American. Women wear fewer slacks, raincoats, and head scarves than in the States. Men's trousers are less colorful and are longer in the leg, and belts are less in evidence.

Feminism is less strong in Britain than in the States, and the women's groups that do exist are often dominated by Americans. On the streets, in advertisements and on British TV you will see more female flesh than in America. The British also tolerate more off-color jokes. America has inherited the Puritan tradition of the emigré Pilgrim Fathers. Remember that the British are descended from the folks who stayed behind.

In Britain, as in much of Europe, safety in public is taken for granted and rarely mentioned. I can't remember ever having heard a British male say that there was somewhere in Britain he wouldn't walk. Unaccompanied women are more careful, though most will walk almost anywhere at any time. Purse-snatching is uncommon in the street, except for two or three areas far from the center of London and also a long way from the districts described in this book. But it's worth guarding against purse thieves on tube platforms; they operate just as the train doors are closing, and distract their victim by jostling her while rifling her purse.

If you go outside London, two points: people walk and perform business transactions more slowly. Second, almost all private farmland is treated as common land, with many "public footpaths" for walking and picnicking. Keep a respectful distance from farm buildings, walk around crops rather than through them, and leave gates as you find them (open or closed). Otherwise, don't be inhibited; for the discreet visitor the British countryside is one great park. Farmers, if you meet them, may well be flattered to have visitors from abroad.

TRANSPORTATION

From Heathrow Airport, think twice about taking a taxi: the cost is high. The underground ("tube" or "underground"—never "subway," which is an underground pedestrian walkway) now connects the airport to central London and most points around the city, and trains leave every few minutes. If you do take a taxi, tell the driver your destination and ask for an estimate of the price before getting in. The driver will probably tell you that the cost of the journey is determined by his meter, but he (usually it's a he) knows roughly what it will be. Settling this beforehand may just save you from an unwanted circular tour. Don't show the driver a map. It probably won't tell him anything about London but it may tell him something about you. Also remember that a taxi's territory is the entire city, and you can't be refused because your destination might be inconvenient. If you have any problems, every taxi has an identification number on the back of the driver's seat; taxi licenses are difficult to come by and most drivers don't want trouble—and won't start it. Except for rare occurrences at airports and other such spots, London taxi drivers on the whole are far more courteous and more knowledgeable about the streets than taxi drivers in most major cities around the world. In central London taxis are often a good value, especially if you have two or three friends with you (the extra cost per person is very small). The taxis to use, if at all possible, are the tall black Austins. Their yellow signs are illuminated when the taxi is available for hire. Unmarked taxis (usually called "minicabs," whatever their size) don't have meters, and the driver charges what he thinks he can get; so it's vital to agree on a price in advance.

Nearly all the public buses in London are the red double-deckers, and from the upper deck you will get some pleasant views. The top deck is also the smoking section. Buses are cheaper than the underground because the service is slower and less reliable. If you are in a hurry, don't trust a bus. (Also remember to line up for the bus; frequently one will pull up and the ticket-taker will say, "One on top, two inside," and only the first three people in the line can board.) But for a romantic, rumbling journey through London on a sunny day, buses are unbeatable. The no. 137 bus, for instance, will take you through the main shopping district (the West End), past Chelsea, across the Thames, through working-class Battersea, and out to the wooded parklands on the southern fringe of London—all for a very low fare. Maps of the bus routes and the underground system are free at tourist bureaus and many underground stations.

The underground is London's main transportation system; it runs from about 6:00 A.M. until midnight. It is noisy, safe, and unromantic—without the frills or rubber wheels of the Paris *métro*. After the morning rush hour, you can get a fairly cheap ticket that allows unlimited journeys for the rest of the day.

Driving in Britain is dangerous and undisciplined compared with the United States. Speed limits—30 mph in town, 70 on motorways and elsewhere—are broken as a matter of course, and drivers change lanes with little or no warning. An American friend, watching with amused horror as a mob of European cars cut across one another, told me, "If you did that in the States, they wouldn't give you a ticket—they'd put you in the clink!" (As an Englishman, my first experience of American roads was one of relief—that I'd escaped from the amateur racetrack of London streets.) Parking space is hard to find in London, and even residents often find that public transportation is not only cheaper than using a car, but also quicker.

HOTELS

Hotels are often more expensive than in the United States, especially when ultramodern. Shared bathrooms are usual (you pay a good deal more for a private bath), and it is unusual to have a television in your room. Don't despise the hotels in Victorian buildings; they are usually cheaper, the service is often good, and the buildings themselves have more character. To British thinking, there is nothing unfashionable about staying in an old hotel; in fact the most chic hotels are rarely modern. West London (around South Kensington and Earl's Court) has many hotels and is much used by visitors. This seems to me a great pity; the area is noisy and restless, and it has prices aimed at the inexperienced visitor. Even the British population here is transient and exploited: secretaries living beyond their means and young accountants shoehorned into partitioned bedrooms. West London may be slightly reassuring, because closer to Heathrow Airport, but I would strongly recommend visitors to look for a hotel in the Russell Square/Bloomsbury area, just to the northeast of central London.

There are large modern hotels close to Russell Square tube station (which is on a direct line to the airport) and smaller hotels in elegant nineteenth-century buildings nearby in the streets by the British Museum (especially in Montague Street and Bedford Place). This district is quieter and cheaper than West London, with older and more attractive buildings. The streets just south of the British Museum have small and slightly bohemian shops and cafés, frequented by museum visitors and staff. Theater-land (around Covent Garden), the main restaurant areas (Soho and Covent Garden), and the chief shopping district (Oxford Street) are all within walking distance. The Russell Square/Bloomsbury area is also handy for four of the five walks in this book.

England is famous for its "bed & breakfast" accommodations (b & b's). In the countryside this means quiet, comfortable rooms in someone's house plus a large English breakfast in the morning, and occasionally before-bed tea. But in London most places that advertise themselves as "b & b's" are really just inexpensive large hotels with little, if any, real personalized hospitality, and a continental breakfast (coffee or tea and a roll with jam), not an English one.

RESTAURANTS AND SHOPS

London has a cosmopolitan population, and for that reason you'll find a huge range of ethnic restaurants. I have included a list of recommended restaurants at the end of the book. Over the years I have been most impressed by two—one Spanish and one Nepalese. In general the British are fond of Chinese, Greek Cypriot, and Indian food; all three kinds are moderately priced. The Chinese dishes and Indian curries are usually hotter than those served in the United States. In an Indian restaurant ask for a mild curry, and be prepared to order yogurt to add to it if you still find it too hot. Good Chinese restaurants cluster in and around Gerrard Street in Soho; a Chinese friend tells me that it's called simply "China Street" by the Chinese themselves. In many restaurants you will have to ask for water; ice water is not generally served.

In British restaurants and shops the consumer does not rule. Customers are often timid, shop assistants and waiters often aloof. The class system is probably at work here; until quite recently the upper class expected deference from staff, who responded by becoming snobs themselves and treating poorer customers accordingly. Waiters and salespeople either dominate or are dominated; there is little democracy. (British people who cross the Atlantic often get a pleasant surprise when they find that American staff regard being friendly as part of the job.) Service in Britain will probably improve if staff pay is drastically increased. Traditionally, shop assistants and waiters are badly paid even by British standards. Consumers themselves are slow to make a fuss, fearing to attract attention and be shown up. The British generally are shy; "I was so embarrassed" is one of the commonest phrases in conversation.

In restaurants, look at the foot of the bill of fare to see whether the service charge is included.

TIPPING

For taxi drivers, 10 to 15 percent; 10 to 15 percent for restaurants with no fixed service charge—unless the service has been poor. The price of a beer for hotel porters. Don't tip theater or cinema attendants unless they've done something very special for you. In greasy-spoon cafés and fish-and-chip shops tips aren't expected, and sometimes the staff won't know how to react if you offer one. In an eating place, a rough guide as to when to tip is: yes, if there's a tablecloth. But there are a few Formica-top-table places which do give restaurant service and where tips are expected.

SHOPPING

The best-known shopping district, Oxford Street, has a branch of the highly reputable Marks and Spencer's (good for clothes). The other very large stores in Oxford Street give reasonable value, but the small shops here have prices aimed at the inexperienced visitor. More interesting are the shops in Covent Garden (reasonable value) and Jermyn Street (expensive), which are mentioned in our first and third walks. Both areas are good for gifts. For inexpensive fresh food, Chapel Market (near Angel tube station) with its open-air stalls is outstanding; it also has a branch of Sainsbury's, Britain's most respected food chain. Middlesex Street ("Petticoat Lane"), close to Liverpool Street tube station, has a famous open-air clothes market on Sunday mornings. It's good for people-watching and for listening to the cheery backchat of the stall-holders, but bargains are few. Look for them instead in the neighboring side streets between Middlesex Street and Brick Lane. For interesting junk and secondhand clothes, Portobello Road (Ladbroke Grove tube station) has a good street market on Saturdays and is popular with young people, who come carefully dressed in the penniless-chic style. Street markets are some of the liveliest and most cheerful places in London; look out, though, for the modern practitioners of the Dickensian tradition of "dipping" (picking pockets). For the addresses of shops and museums, don't forget that London's most useful book is the telephone directory.

PUBS

Here London excels, the pubs often being works of art in themselves with their elaborate plaster ceilings, woodwork and mirrors. The atmosphere is usually relaxed and democratic, and unaccompanied women go in as a matter of course. There used to be a protocol in pubs that kept locals and the lower classes in a "Public Bar" area, middle and upper classes in a "Private Bar" area, and men and women together in a "Saloon Bar." These distinctions don't mean much today (especially in central London) but some signs for them still exist, and there are certain neighborhood pubs where these and other protocols are followed to some extent (some interesting Cockney pubs of Southwark among them, but mostly out in the country—where, by and large, the best, most atmospheric pubs are). Pubs are not recognized pickup places; singles bars are virtually unknown in Britain. Heavy drinking is unusual; far more often, pubs are used for making business deals or for spending an evening with friends. Prices in central London pubs vary only slightly; if a Londoner says that a pub is expensive, all that's meant is that beer is a few pence more per pint than elsewhere.

Beer generally is served by gas pressure and, apart from lager, is darker and sweeter than most American brews. Since the early 1970s gassed beer has been the target of one of Britain's very few consumer revolts—the Campaign for Real Ale. The beer served by use of carbon dioxide is biochemically dead, usually short on alcohol, and needs little or no skill to serve. The big brewing corporations, which own most pubs, adopted it soon after the Second World War, claiming that bar staff were incapable of serving the traditional beer properly. Traditional beer (Real Ale) is flat, contains living yeast, is often strong, and is served by hand pump after maturing in the pub's cellar. The Campaign for Real Ale, made up largely of young middle-class men, attacks the Big Bad Brewers and champions the small companies that have persevered with traditional beer. In London it has been highly successful, forcing the big corporations to remove some of their plastic-pump displays and fizzy beer and to replace them with the vertical hand pumps and Real Ale. The most respected brewery in London is the small firm of Young's, which produces consistently excellent Real Ale from a brewery in a South London farmyard. Much of it is then delivered by horse-drawn wagon.

CINEMAS

The large cinemas show mainly the latest popular films from America. But scattered around London is a rich variety of classic, avant-garde, and foreign-language films. Tracking them down, often in unfamiliar parts of London and sometimes late at night, is a favorite adventure of Londoners themselves. For details of programs, see the next section.

ENTERTAINMENTS

The best general guide is a weekly magazine called *What's On*. The magazines *Time Out* and *City Limits* are similar, but have an uneasy editorial mixture of trendiness and radicalism and are written in a mid-Atlantic style. However, both are good for details of foreign-language and avant-garde films.

NEWSPAPERS

Perhaps the best guide to England's news publications is the following well-known, pithy characterization.

"The *Financial Times* is read by the people who own the country; the *Times* by the people who run the country. The *Daily Mail* is read by the wives of the people who run the country; the *Guardian* by liberals who *think* they run the country. The *Daily Telegraph* is read by the people who used to run the country [ex-officers, elderly aristocrats]; the *Daily Express* by people who want the Queen to run the country. The *Daily Mirror* is read by people who want the unions to run the country; the [Communist] *Morning Star* is read by people who wanted another country to run the country; the [mildly pornographic] *Sun* is read by people who don't care who runs the country so long as she has big tits."

There's also the magazine *Private Eye*, a bold mixture of esoteric satire and straight exposé.

ASKING FOR INFORMATION

In choosing local people to approach for information, look for someone who doesn't seem in a hurry. A working-class person of fifty or older is often a good bet, because he or she may well have lived in the area for many years. "Working class" in Britain does not mean "poor"; most of the population is working class. A working-class person, roughly speaking, is someone who does a nonprofessional job, has a local accent, and does not have a college education. One of the best-informed Londoners I have met was an elderly porter, sitting on a fruit barrow amid the picturesque grime of Whitechapel. Working-class men like this may take pride, patronizing but friendly, in answering your questions. The women, in my experience, know just as much but are more modest and also have a nicer sense of humor. On a bus I once overheard two working-class, middle-aged London women talking about marriage and True Love. "Well," said one of them with resigned cheerfulness, "I don't know about True Love, but he'll be lucky to find another old donkey to work for him like I have!" If you ask for information from a group of women in a street market or a party of women office workers, you may well find yourself getting advice and good-humored jokes for several minutes.

HELP

Visitors who are seriously injured or contract infectious diseases can get free treatment under the National Health Service when taken to the casualty department of a hospital. Not every hospital has a casualty department; of those that do, University College Hospital (Gower Street, WC1, tel. 387-9300) has a fine reputation.

Boots, a large drugstore at Piccadilly Circus, fills pre-scriptions from 8:30 A.M. to 8:00 P.M. (Closed Sundays; on Sundays other drugstores stay open in rotation; a call to the local police station will tell you which.) (Drug-stores are called "chemists"; those that fill prescriptions are called "dispensing chemists.") The three emergency services—fire, ambulance and police—are reached by di-alling 999 from any phone.

For other serious problems, the American Embassy is at 24 Grosvenor Square, W1 (Bond Street tube station), tel. 499-9000. The Canadian High Commission is in Tra-falgar Square, tel. 629-9492; and the Australian High Commission is in The Strand, WC2, tel. 438-8000.

TELEPHONES

Public phone booths are of two types; one takes coins, the other takes cards. These phonecards can be bought in many newspaper stores and allow you to make inter-national as well as local calls.

You can dial direct to anywhere in the States (dial 0101 and then the American codes). A minute's call will cost only a few dollars, even to the West Coast.

Glossary

AMERICAN	BRITISH
Subway	Tube, underground ("Subway" in Britain means a tunnel for pedes-trians under a main road.)
Excuse me	Sorry ("Excuse me" in Britain means "Please let me through.")

Pants	Trousers ("Pants" in Britain usually means "underclothes.")
Check (in restaurant)	Bill
Restroom, washroom, bathroom	If in public ask for "the ladies" or "the gents" ("Is there a ladies near here?"). In a private house, ask for "the bathroom" or "the loo." "Restroom" will probably not be understood.
Line (of people)	Queue
Two-lane (in same direction)	Dual carriageway
Gasoline	Petrol
Trunk (of an automobile)	Boot
Windshield	Windscreen
Highway	Motorway (marked by signs)
Call collect	Reverse the charges
Busy signal (on telephone)	Engaged tone
Drugstore	Chemist (A dispensing chemist fills prescriptions.)
Sidewalk	Pavement
Traffic circle	Roundabout
Do you have . . . ?	Have you got . . . ?
Gotten	Got
Truck	Lorry
One-way ticket	Single ticket ("Birmingham, single, please.")
Round-trip ticket	Return ticket (Going to and from on the same day, which is often much cheaper, is called a "cheap day return.")
Here or to go?	Eat here or take away?
First floor	Ground floor ("First floor" in Britain means the second story, "second floor" means the third story, and so on.)

Elevator	Lift
Apartment	Flat
Coffee with cream	White coffee
Dessert	Sweet, pudding
Legal holiday	Bank holiday
Two weeks	Fortnight (14 nights)

SLANG	EQUIVALENT
Quid, nicker	Pound (money; written "Two quid," "Three nicker")
Five "p," ten "p," etc.	Five pence, ten pence, etc.
Grotty	Dirty, unattractive
Custom (as in "Thank you for your custom.")	Patronage
Fag	Cigarette
Cheers	Thanks, good-bye
Ta (pronounced "tah")	Thanks
Mate	Friend
Bird	Girl, woman (a mildly sexist term)
Bloody	An all-purpose swear word; mild but not for polite company
Stroppy	Indignant, making trouble
All at sea	In difficulties, confused

Tea will come with milk, unless you ask clearly for lemon tea. The word *street* is almost never dropped from the title of a British road; if you ask for Oxford when you are in central London, you'll probably be directed to the city of Oxford, not Oxford Street.

A few final pieces of advice. When you find places that you like, go back to them several times if possible. Repetition helps memory; that way you'll get a photograph in your mind, better than one on film. For finding your way around the areas of London not covered here, I recommend buying the inexpensive book of maps called

A to Z (*Z* is pronounced "zed" in Britain), which is on sale at many newsstands. Its index is excellent, and often vital for Londoners themselves. It covers all of London—in sections. When meeting British people, remember that occupation more than money determines someone's social class in Britain, so it is not polite to ask directly what job a person does. Don't be put off by the rather reserved British manner. Many British people have come to appreciate American openness and friendliness, and a slight smile or gleam in the eye of a British person can mean "I like you very much."

Walk · 1

The London Dickens Knew

ADELPHI AND

COVENT GARDEN

WALK 1: Adelphi and Covent Garden

Starting Point: Embankment tube station
Buses: 109, 155, 184

When England emerged from the Middle Ages, there were two cities on the north bank of the lower Thames: the City of London and the City of Westminster. They stood within a couple of miles of each other. The City of London, to the east, was the older, built over the site of Roman Londinium. The Romans themselves hadn't originally intended London to be their capital in Britain; that was to be Camulodunum (now Colchester), more than forty miles away to the northeast. But because they hated seafaring, the Romans weren't willing to sail directly from the Continent to Camulodunum; instead, they landed on the Channel coast and marched toward it, crossing the Thames by bridge at the point where it ceased to be tidal. At the northern end of that bridge traders settled to exploit the traffic, and there Londinium grew up. By A.D. 100 the new settlement had overtaken Camulodunum and become the chief town of Britain.

Roman troops left Britain soon after A.D. 400 to defend richer parts of their crumbling empire. Many centuries later, the Roman walls of London were patched and raised to protect the medieval city. Inside the walls traders and financiers were able to negotiate with monarchs from a position of strength; kings of England normally ruled from Westminster, and thought twice about entering the City of London. As late as the nineteenth century the unpopular King George IV dared not go in for fear of physical attack.

When Londoners say "the City" they still mean the traditional City of London on, or very close to, its Roman site. The City keeps its own Lord Mayor, local government, and police; it is also still the headquarters of private finance. Government, too, has stayed in its old place, at Westminster, and goes on dealing cautiously with the financiers down the river. So the tradition of two cities is still alive.

On a later walk (#2) we shall be going inside the western boundary of the City of London. But this walk will be in Westminster, starting on the Embankment, a piece of land reclaimed from the river in the 1860s. Both parts of our route, the Adelphi and Covent Garden, were well known to Dickens. His father worked nearby as a government clerk, and Dickens himself played here as a child. When his father was imprisoned for debt in 1824, Dickens was put to work in a neighboring factory—at the age of twelve.

In the Adelphi district, most of the streets were laid out in the seventeenth and eighteenth centuries. Several of the original houses survive. The Adelphi itself, as we shall see, was an elegant—and desperate—piece of speculative building by the Adam brothers. (*Adelphi* is Greek for "brothers," and punned on the architects' name.) It was begun in 1768. Today its dignified streets are quiet, and on weekends you'll have the place largely to yourself. But in Dickens's day the area was crowded; riverboats put in at the Adelphi, and their passengers were plundered along the waterfront by a gang of child thieves.

North of the Adelphi is a main road, **The Strand.** Its name originally meant "the shore"—the river once ran that close. After crossing The Strand, you will reach **Covent Garden** by a set of dark alleys. Quite safe these days, in the nineteenth century these alleys were a refuge for criminals; they still have the Victorian gaslights that were installed to prevent dark deeds. In Covent Garden itself, dozens of gaslights—some of delicate design, others set on massive iron brackets—are still working. In the Middle Ages the place was a convent garden, but after Henry VIII confiscated the property of the Catholic religious orders in the 1530s, the land passed to the Earls (later Dukes) of Bedford. They owned it until 1914, when the 11th Duke sold the entire estate and used much of the proceeds to make what seemed to be a far safer investment—in Russian government bonds. These, of course, collapsed during the revolution three years later.

Much earlier, in the 1630s, the 4th Earl of Bedford had hired the court architect, Inigo Jones, to turn Covent Garden into a grand suburb with Italianate buildings. Although Jones's work in the area has now entirely disappeared, its influence remains, especially in the stylish Central Market buildings constructed in 1830 for the sale of fruit and vegetables. This market trade, already centuries old, was to remain here until 1974, when it was transferred to a site south of the Thames. Now that the fruit and vegetable trucks have gone, Covent Garden is delightfully free of traffic, like a stillness at the center of the whirlpool of London.

In the evenings, Covent Garden is a middle-class playground—for the hip, the radical, and the genteel. A few yards from the Royal Opera House, loud rock music rises from the cellars and from behind the shutters of former vegetable stores. In the daytime, numerous small and unusual shops are run by proud specialists. And for centuries Covent Garden has been the most important place in Britain for authors and publishers to socialize and do business. In the pubs, editors swap horror stories of unreliable authors and authors tell of royalties never seen. Dickens edited a magazine in Covent Garden toward the end of his life, and ate at the best restaurant here. (It still survives, as we shall see.) Many years earlier, in the 1820s, he had wandered in the area as an impoverished child, staring hungrily at the pineapples in the market.

Embankment tube station has two exits; take the one on the left as you come from the ticket barrier, and walk along the right-hand side of the road which runs straight towards you—**Villiers Street**. The people selling flowers and newspapers here live on the small river of commuters and pleasure-seekers running from the tube to the great railway terminal of Charing Cross at the other end of Villiers Street and to theater-land, one-quarter of a mile beyond.

As you walk away from the tube, with the grim railway bridge on your left, you'll see a pleasant park on your right that is a traditional refuge for a few derelicts. In his book *Down and Out in Paris and London*, George Orwell describes sleeping here himself in the 1930s while living as a vagrant and exploring poverty from the inside. Judging by their accents, the derelicts gathered here nowadays are mostly from northeastern England, Scotland, and Ireland. I haven't heard many accents from London or the Midlands, which are more prosperous areas, or from Wales, which is poor but with a strong temperance tradition.

Walk 50 yards along Villiers Street; where the park ends, on the right, is a tiny and eccentric old building, standing alone—one room, a basement and a tall chimney. It is still in use, as a shop for shoe repair. In a moment, when you go down the steps right next to this building, look back and you will see that it leans strongly to the north.

The little building happens to mark the line of the old Thames waterfront, before the Embankment was made. The park (called Victoria Embankment Gardens)

Miniature memorial to Imperial Camel Corps,
Victoria Embankment Gardens

and the tube station stand where there was once river, or river-mud. The massive building on the left of Villiers Street is **Charing Cross Station,** constructed partly over the new Embankment in the mid-1860s. It stands over the site of the decrepit shoe-blacking factory where Dickens worked as a child.

He later wrote about the factory and his dreary work in it: "It was a crazy tumbledown old house, abutting of course on the river, and literally overrun with rats. . . . My work was to cover the pots of paste blacking first with a piece of oil paper, and then with a piece of blue paper, to tie them round with string, and then to clip the paper close to them making it neat all round." Dickens's point about rats is probably not an exaggeration. The rat had a great time in nineteenth-century London. One music hall of the period was praised because ladies could sit in it *without* being overrun by rats.

Go down the steps beside the little crooked building into the passageway called **Watergate Walk.** This was the waterfront of the Thames until the 1860s. You'll see the great stone water gate about 50 yards from the steps, on the right. Ten yards along from the foot of the steps, on the left, there was—until 1990—the entrance to a much-loved and discreet London meeting place in an old cellar, Gordon's winebar. Its door had dingy paint and carried no name. It was designed not to attract casual trade. Through the door lay a steep set of irregular stone steps. Falling down these was a sign that someone didn't belong. Gordon's closed much earlier than most winebars, at nine. Any later, presumably, and the proportion of stumbling customers might have become slightly worrying. From the steps alone a social historian could have guessed that England is not a litigious country. The first impulse of many English people, on having an accident, is to be apologetic rather than to blame others. (Unless they're driving, that is; in Britain motoring transcends morality.) The whole ramshackle arrangement of Gordon's lamented cellar, with its vaulted roof, its flickering candles, and the prosperous young civil servants with a reason not to go home, depended on word of mouth. To have found your way there at all was as good as an introduction to the other customers. The bar staff, unusually for a large city, scarcely changed for years on end, and knew the "regulars"—if they wanted to be known. Journalists in the national press came to the defense of Gordon's when the business fought its last battle, against a huge rent rise.

Bottom-line values may have triumphed here. But in London generally, would-be *demolishers* of interesting buildings have quite a hard time. Any citizen can alert the authorities to a structure that may deserve legal protection; the building need be no more than a few decades old. Overnight, unsuspecting owners find that their property has, in the British phrase, "had a Preservation Order slapped on it." Then a common compromise is to preserve the façaade and modernize the interior. Alternatively, sometimes there are fires, or demolition a few hours before a legal order to preserve comes into effect. A few years ago, a famous building from the 1930s, the Firestone tire factory in west London, was about to be preserved by the minister for the environment, Michael Heseltine. The requisite paper was on his desk, waiting for signature. But there was a leak to the owners, who then demolished within hours. The story goes that Heseltine in consequence was so angry that he asked the relevant conservation group, the Thirties Society, to supply him with a long list of sites that they valued and then signed Preservation Orders for the lot.

Go a few yards farther along the path to the **York Watergate.** This hefty triple structure in yellow stone was built in the mid-1620s. It led to a private quay, which stood out over the Thames mud, allowing favored people to land without getting dirty. The water gate was built for one of the most colorful and disastrous figures of the early seventeenth century, George Villiers, Duke of Buckingham. Buckingham's grand residence, York House, stood where Gordon's once was, and his gardens stretched across the site of the present Buckingham Street.

Born in 1592, George Villiers was to become the favorite first of King James I and then of James's son, Charles I. Although not of aristocratic family, he shot up in the court hierarchy (due to his good looks, popular belief had it) and was promoted within eight years to viscount, earl, marquis, and finally duke. King James clumsily defended his support of Buckingham thus: "You may be sure that I love the Earl of Buckingham more than anyone else . . . Christ had his John, and I have my George." By 1625, when James died and was succeeded by Charles, Buckingham had become virtually ruler of England.

Buckingham used his power with an appalling lack of skill. In 1623 he and Charles had gone to Spain to arrange a marriage between Charles and the Spanish princess. The attempt failed, and Buckingham insulted the Spanish court. Later he also insulted the court of France by making amorous advances in public to their queen. In a war with France shortly thereafter, Buckingham led a naval expedition against French forces at La Rochelle; he was defeated and lost most of his men. Parliament bitterly objected to Buckingham's power and tried to impeach him. Enough anonymous poems were written against him to fill a small book. Buckingham took part in a ballet here at York House; the following is a poem contrasting the stern English warriors of old with this dancing courtier who attempted to fight the French.

> *Rejoice, brave English gallants,*
> *whose ancestors won France,*
> *Our Duke of Buckingham is gone*
> *to fight and not to dance.*
> *Believe it; for our ladies*
> *his absence greatly mourn;*
> *And swear they'll have no babies*
> *until he doth return.*

One unofficial notice about Buckingham was nailed up in the City of London: "Who rules the kingdom? The King. Who rules the King? The Duke. Who rules the Duke? The Devil. Let the Duke look to it." This was slang, meaning "He'd better watch out." Buckingham did not "look to it" with enough care. In 1628, while preparing another foreign military adventure, he was stabbed in the chest by an aggrieved ex–naval officer. He called out "Villain," staggered, and died. King Charles blamed Parliament for encouraging Buckingham's assassin. Their quarrel helped lead eventually to the Civil Wars of the 1640s and to Charles's own violent death on the scaffold at Whitehall.

Buckingham's water gate reflects his career. He lived on this site only because he had unscrupulously evicted the previous occupant of York House, the philosopher and politician Francis Bacon. Above the two outer bays of the gate, visible from Watergate Walk, are stones carved in the shape of anchors. These were meant to remind people of Buckingham's role as admiral. His coat of arms, over the central arch, has a duke's coronet shown above it to advertise his social success. The inscription in Latin, which runs across all three bays, is Buckingham's pious family motto, *Fidei Coticula Crux* ("The cross is the touchstone of faith"). To see how the gate was meant to look from the river, either go through it, or, if it's locked, go around into the park by way of the entrance which is just the other side of the crooked house. The water gate was designed in an Italian style, which was the one approved by the court at the time. On the river side it has attached columns with artificially roughened bands. This rustication is an Italian device to make architecture look countrified.

York House itself was sold in the early 1670s by Buckingham's son, the 2nd Duke. It was demolished shortly afterwards, and streets were laid out over the site. Of the home of the scandalous Buckingham, only his water gate now remains.

Go up the double set of steps just opposite the water gate into **Buckingham Street.** The first building on the right **(nos. 15–16)** is the only modern one in the street. It stands on the site of a house where Dickens lived briefly as a young journalist in 1834 and which he used as part of the setting of *David Copperfield.* Dickens's houses in London, like this one in Buckingham Street, have nearly all been destroyed. The one important house left, in Doughty Street (near Chancery Lane tube station), is kept as a Dickens museum.

The seventeenth- and eighteenth-century houses in Buckingham Street are tall and mostly flat-fronted. The best rooms—those with the tallest windows and highest ceilings—are on the second story.* Look across the street at **no. 11.** The grand second-story rooms were designed to be as different as possible from the servants' quarters. Servants lived under the roof, with small windows—and the noise of the pigeons. The master and his family avoided living on the top floor because that was the most dangerous place in the event of a fire.

This street was begun less than ten years after the Great Fire of 1666, in which most of the City of London was destroyed. For the builders of Buckingham Street fire prevention was definitely a consideration—even so, several of the houses did eventually burn down (nos. 13 and 14 in 1684 and no. 19 in 1794).

Outside **no. 18** are traces of elegant living—and of fire precautions—from the 1700s: hollow cones of iron, set on a frame on each side of the door. The cones, called "link extinguishers," were used at night to put out torches (links). Until the coming of gas lighting, in the early nineteenth century, link boys were hired to run, torches blazing, in front of a carriage to guide it past potholes and obstacles. Crime flourished in the dark streets; the link boys, in reality often men, were also meant to serve as a

---

*British usage for referring to floors of buildings is employed throughout. See page 16.

defense against robbery. Once the passengers had alighted, the torches—commonly made with tar or candle wax—were extinguished by being thrust into the iron cones. (The link boys would have put out their torches anyway for the sake of economy, and if they did so by trampling them on the ground a fire might have broken out in the litter in the street.) Link extinguishers were also a sign that you were expecting grand guests, the sort who could afford a carriage and link boys. Many of the surviving eighteenth- and early-nineteenth-century houses in London were originally artisans' dwellings and have been revamped in recent years. But link extinguishers show that a house was already a grand residence more than 150 years ago.

Notice the light—the small window directly above the door—at no. 18; it is divided by strips of metal in the shape of a fan. Traditionally, different houses on a street had different lights, perhaps for purposes of identification before house numbers came into use. No. 13, across the street, has a different style of fanlight; no. 17's light is in a diamond pattern.

From 1697, **no. 13** was the home of Dr. William Coward, a well-known religious heretic. Coward argued that the soul was never separated from the body, and that soul and body would rise together at the resurrection. Today it might be difficult to find Christians sure that this doctrine *is* heretical, let alone why it is. But in Coward's day interest in Protestant theology was intense. In 1704 the House of Commons discussed his writings and ordered them to be burned by the common hangman, a practice both humiliating and frightening to the writer. Of course it also increased public interest in Coward's books.

Samuel Pepys lived for nine years, starting in 1679, at **no. 12** Buckingham Street, and the house has changed little since his day. In England, because of his delightful diary, Pepys's name is probably the best known of any English writer between the times of Shakespeare and

Dickens. The main diary runs from 1660 to 1669, when Pepys was in his twenties and thirties, and before he lived in Buckingham Street. It shows him to have been a man of unusual self-awareness. Like Dickens, Pepys had great energy for both work and women. His diary gives lively backstairs details about Charles II's court and about Pepys's own home.

As a boy, Pepys had seen the execution of Charles I and had definitely approved. In the 1660s, with the dead King's son, Charles II, on the throne, he was frightened that someone would remember this. Nevertheless, he quietly kept some republican sympathies and was upset by the punishment of Charles I's old enemies: "This afternoon . . . I saw the limbs of some of our new traitors set upon Aldersgate in the City of London, which was a sad sight to see; and a bloody week this and the last have been, there being ten hanged, drawn and quartered."

Pepys got his first post in Charles II's civil service through the influence of a relative. He admitted to himself that he had depended on nepotism, and needed to work hard to survive: "Chance without merit brought me in, and diligence only keeps me so, and will [do], living as I do among so many lazy people that the diligent man becomes necessary, that they cannot do anything without him." But he explained to himself why pleasure, too, was needed: "The truth is, I do indulge myself a little more in pleasure, knowing that this is the proper age of my life to do it [he was in his early thirties at the time]; and, out of my observation that most men that do thrive in the world do forget to take pleasure during the time they are getting their estate, but reserve that till they have got one, and then it is too late for them to enjoy it."

Pepys thought the King had a bit too much pleasure with the royal mistresses: "The King do spend most of his time in feeling and kissing them naked . . . this lechery will never leave him." But Pepys took similar pleasures. When he fell in love with his maid, Deb Willett, his wife found out and there were great quarrels. Once

Mrs. Pepys got so angry that "she came to my side of the bed and drew my curtain open, and with the tongs, red hot at the ends, made as if she did design to pinch me with them." But he shrewdly noticed that this quarrel about Deb improved his marital relations in one way: "I have lain with my *moher* ["wife" in Spanish] as a husband more times since this falling-out than in, I believe, twelve months before—and with more pleasure to her than, I think, in all the time of our marriage before."

For much of his life Pepys was the most important administrator of the British navy. He became rich, partly by using—or abusing—his power to award contracts. But he describes one bribe which he did not want: some expensive fish, sent to persuade him to accept overpriced tar from a Mr. Bowyer. Pepys decided to say no to Mr. Bowyer, though he received "last night, as a bribe, a barrel of sturgeon, which, it may be, I shall send back, for I will not have the King abused so abominably in the price of what we buy . . ."

In May 1679, during an anti-Catholic panic, Pepys was accused of leaking information about the navy to the government of Catholic France and of plotting against Protestantism. He was locked up for a time in the Tower of London, but the prosecution case collapsed. Pepys was released and given even more power over naval affairs. It was at about this time that he first came to live in Buckingham Street. From no. 12 he ran the navy. In 1688 he moved just down the street to a grander house, which has not survived but which stood on the site of the present no. 14.

That same year, after a reign of only three years, Charles II's Catholic brother James II was driven out of England by a Protestant invasion. This was bad news for Pepys, who had been given the job of organizing James's navy to keep the invaders out. Since Pepys was suspected of remaining secretly loyal to the exiled James, he was imprisoned in 1689, under the new King, William III. But he was soon released, and although he lost his control of the navy, he seems to have ended his life a popular man. Until 1701 (two years before his death) he remained owner of the house that stood down by the water gate.

At the top of Buckingham Street turn right into **John Adam Street** and walk to the next corner on the right (where John Adam Street joins York Buildings). You are now on the edge of the **Adelphi,** the streets created by Robert, James, and William Adam between 1768 and 1774. Their designs were inspired by fine Italian houses. Look ahead of you, to the very end of John Adam Street. The house facing down the street was decorated by the brothers with especially bold lines; it was meant to be impressive at a distance to people coming up John Adam Street, as you're doing now. From here you can see that it has four tall pilasters in its façade—flat-fronted columns built into the brick. Soon after they were finished, the Adelphi buildings were berated by a writer who said they were "warehouses, laced down the seams," and looked like a soldier's tart dressed in a regimental coat. This was harsh criticism, but seeing the house from a distance helps to explain it.

When the brothers began to build here, the land sloped very steeply down to the Thames. So Robert Adam, the chief architect, lessened the gradient by building great rows of arches to support his streets as they approached the river. These arches were extremely expensive, and in 1773, before the Adelphi was finished, the Adams' funds ran out. A vast lottery was held to raise money to complete the project; over 4,300 tickets were issued at £50 each. The prizes were to be the houses, warehouses, shops and storage vaults of the Adelphi. Fifty pounds was a large sum at that time; eighty years later common soldiers were earning less than £20 a year. But gambling was highly popular with the middle and upper classes in eighteenth-century England, and many of the tickets were no doubt bought by syndicates. Some of the winners quickly sold their prizes, and thus could divide their winnings.

Dickens wrote in *David Copperfield*: "I was fond of

Brass knocker, door of Royal Society of Arts

wandering about the Adelphi, because it was a mysterious place with those dark arches." The centerpiece of the Adams' scheme, Adelphi Terrace, was demolished in the 1930s and most of the arches are gone. But you can still see one: turn into the street called York Buildings and 15 yards along go left into **Lower Robert Street**, which dives underground; it may look grim but it is quite safe. There's no proper sidewalk, so watch out for the cars which swoop up and down here. Just after you go underground, and before turning to the right, you'll pass under one of the original dark arches.

Go under the arch, turn right and head for the daylight about 100 yards ahead. It was from tunnels like this, underneath the Adelphi, that the child thieves operated in the early 1840s. The children specialized in stealing expensive silk handkerchiefs from gentlemen's coattail pockets. One thief, who was interviewed as an adult in the early 1860s, told a story very much like that of Dickens's *Oliver Twist*. He had run away to London at the age of nine and gone to live in a slum at Field Lane—an evil street, now demolished, west of St. Paul's Cathedral. Later he joined the child thieves here at the Adelphi, sleeping with them in a derelict van under the arches. Their thief-master was named not Fagin but Larry, and he threatened those children who did not bring him their stolen handkerchiefs with disclosure to the police. Only those who obeyed him were allowed to sleep in the van.

Dickens's *Oliver Twist* was realistic about the way many stray children were forced to live in early-nineteenth-century England. Easy to frighten and control, these urchins were useful to thief-masters: their touch for picking pockets was more delicate than that of most adults; police were hesitant to arrest small children; and, even if caught and convicted, children were less likely than adults to be transported to Australia.

On leaving the underground road, you'll come out into York Place, once the waterfront and now hemmed in with gardens. Go up the steps that begin a few feet away to your left. At the top is a large office block of the 1930s. It is out of scale with the Adam streets around it, and its masses of glass and concrete clash with the delicate decoration of the eighteenth-century buildings. Look up at the art deco designs, the emphatic verticals and the overpowering statues, fit for a dictator's palace. The architects of the office block— Collcutt and Hamp—made way for their scheme by knocking down the Adelphi Terrace, which was the heart of the eighteenth-century Adelphi.

Turn your back to the offices, and look out over the low wall towards the river. Below you is a pleasant view of the park on the Thames Embankment. In the 1860s, the novelist Thomas Hardy trained as an architect here in Adelphi Terrace and watched the Embankment being built. He later used his knowledge of architecture to create the character of George Somerset, the architect-hero of *A Laodicean* (one of the very few of Hardy's novels that does not end in tragedy).

Through the trees to the left, at the river's edge, you can see the top of Cleopatra's Needle, the ancient Egyptian obelisk which was set up on the Embankment in 1878. Some mementos of the 1870s were buried beneath it, including Bradshaw's Railway Timetable and portraits of Lillie Langtry, the mistress of the heir to the throne. More on her in a little while.

Walk the 100 yards or so of Robert Street, with its Adam houses on the left and Collcutt and Hamp on the right. When you reach the corner with John Adam Street you will see, slightly to the right, perhaps the prettiest section of the whole Adelphi scheme: the home of the **Royal Society of Arts.** It would make a lovely advertisement for Britain as many of the British would like it to appear.

The doorway of the building, which dates from 1774, is decorated with string-molding, almost a trademark of Robert Adam's work. Above the doorway is a large window, fan-shaped at the top in a Venetian style. Miniature Ionic Greek columns on each side of the window help to divide the façade. And to prevent a feeling of heaviness in the pediment (the shallow triangle under the roof), Adam included a small, circular window to break up the expanse of brickwork.

The Royal Society of Arts was founded in 1754 to encourage inventors. It still does. A gold medal was recently awarded here to an engineer, Eric Donald, who had designed an aircraft bolt to give early warning of metal fatigue. The bolt is hollow and filled with dye; if it cracks it "bleeds" visibly onto the surface of the plane. The presentation of the medal here brought important

Adelphi

early publicity for the invention. So Robert Adam's elegant building is still doing its job.

Pass the front of the building, and go a few yards, to the corner of Adam Street. **No. 7** Adam Street is the building you noticed a while ago from a distance. From here you can see that the pilasters and door frame have an intricate set of moldings. Adam decoration like this, especially string-moldings around fireplaces and doors, later became highly fashionable; connoisseurs of late-eighteenth-century buildings still look eagerly for it. But, at the time, many architects found the style effeminate and silly. One of them, Sir William Chambers, who preferred a simpler and more massive style of building, is said to have persuaded King George III not to give Robert Adam a knighthood. Shortly after the building of the Adelphi, Chambers put up one of his own portly constructions close by, no doubt expecting people to see its superiority. This was Somerset House, a set of government buildings, which still stands (with additions) about 300 yards east of the Adelphi. It was in Somerset House that Dickens's imprudent father worked as a clerk in the Admiralty.

No. 8 Adam Street, with its fine doorcase, was owned from 1788 to 1792 by Richard Arkwright, one of the pioneers of the Industrial Revolution. Arkwright's great invention was the spinning frame, a machine that used the power of water or steam to convert raw cotton into thread. He made a fortune by exploiting this invention in factories in the north of England. His competitors copied it, and Arkwright probably took this expensive town house for its nearness to the London courts, where he spent much time defending his legal rights as inventor.

About 40 yards to the north Adam Street ends at The Strand—a traffic-ridden highway between Westminster and the City. Cross The Strand at the pedestrian crossing a few yards to the left. (A child recently described pedestrian crossings rather well: "They're places where cars aren't allowed to knock you down.") When you are across the street, look right, toward the City, at the two fine churches that stand in the middle of the road, one behind the other, like islands in the river of steel. The nearer one is **St. Mary's-le-Strand** (Dickens's parents were married here in 1809). The French *le* in the name is a trace of the last conquest of England; William of Normandy and his associates, who captured England in 1066, spoke French, and French remained the everyday language of the court for over three centuries. The church farther away is **St. Clement Danes,** badly bombed in the last war but now restored to the seventeenth-century design of Christopher Wren. This is the church mentioned in the traditional nursery rhyme about London bells:

"Oranges and lemons," say the bells of St. Clement's,
"You owe me five farthings," say the bells of St. Martin's,
"When will you pay me?" say the bells of Old Bailey,
"When I am rich," say the bells of Shoreditch.

About a yard from the end of the pedestrian crossing, to the left, there's an entrance to an alley, **Exchange Court.** Walking up the alley, you will come to your first Covent Garden gaslight. In the daytime the timing mechanism ticks away unnoticed, just a few yards from the modern noise of The Strand.

Gas lighting became common in London around 1820 and was only slowly squeezed out by electric lighting at the end of the century. In 1878 gas stocks crashed on the London exchange; people thought that the age of electricity had already arrived. But the shares soon made a comeback. For one thing, poor people were reluctant to part with their gaslights because they gave out a slight heat. Also, by the end of the nineteenth century, the newest types of gaslight were so bright that, for street lighting, there wasn't much difference between them and electricity. Perhaps the main reason for their eventual disuse was the cost of the labor needed to maintain them.

Victorian writers themselves, as well as modern filmmakers, have used gas lighting as a romantic setting. This sentimental song is about a Victorian flower-seller:

> *Underneath the gaslight's glitter*
> *Stands a little, fragile girl,*
> *Heedless of the night winds bitter*
> *As they round about her whirl;*
>
> *While the hundreds pass unheeding*
> *In the evening's waning hours,*
> *Still she cries, with tearful pleading,*
> *"Won't you buy my pretty flowers?"*

Moving stuff! Victorian writers loved children—especially when they were dying.

The reason for installing gaslights in the first place was not at all sentimental. In 1823 the parish of Hampstead bought gaslights for its own streets because they were "the most efficient aid to the police in the repression and detection of offenders in the streets and highways." And in these grim passages north of The Strand it is easy to see why.

Fifty yards up the alley you will see Maiden Lane. On the way there, look over the wall on the left or through the grille in its gate at the backs of tall, bleak nineteenth-century slums.

When the alley emerges into **Maiden Lane**, turn right. A few yards along on the right, where the road widens slightly, are the rear doors of the **Adelphi Theatre**. (Its entrance is on The Strand.) Above the first door is a crude molding of the royal coat of arms. This "royal entrance" is used as a stage door, and in 1897 it was the scene of a famous murder. William Terriss, a leading actor of the period, was entering the theater one night by the stage door when he was stabbed to death. The killer, a minor actor, seems to have believed insanely that, with Terriss dead, he himself could become famous in Terriss's place. He was arrested, raving, a few yards away in

Maiden Lane, and only his madness saved him from the scaffold. The ghost of William Terriss features in some of the more interesting stories of Covent Garden hauntings. Many ghost stories from this area originate with actors, and you can't help wondering how many of them have merely been testing their acting skills by trying to convince people of spooky nonsense. But in 1955 two rather more believable people, workers at Covent Garden tube station, were separately frightened by the figure of a man with old-fashioned clothes and pale gloves. One of them said he had tried to question the man, who then vanished in front of his eyes. The other, when shown a photo of Terriss, is said to have claimed immediately that this was the person he had seen.

A few yards farther down Maiden Lane, on the other side, is **no. 35, Rule's restaurant.** Inside, the dining rooms are still furnished in their Victorian style. Paintings and prints from the nineteenth century cover most of the walls; and there is a gleam of dark wood from the sideboards and chairs. Dickens used to visit Rule's in the last years of his life. Tradition has it that his favorite table was in an alcove at the rear of the second story. The alcove is out of the sight of most of the diners, so this would certainly have been a good place for the famous author to find some privacy.

In the 1870s the restaurant was a favorite of the Prince of Wales, later to become King Edward VII. His special table was in the alcove at the front of the second story, by the window at the far right (looking from the street). Edward used to come here with his mistress, Lillie Langtry. He was already married and had children (one of whom, incidentally, was later to be suspected of being Jack the Ripper, the murderer of 1888; see pages 116–17), so Edward, understandably, was very anxious for privacy when dining here à deux with Lillie. His alcove was curtained off, and a special doorway was built that enabled him to enter the alcove without being seen by other diners. The curtain has been removed, but the

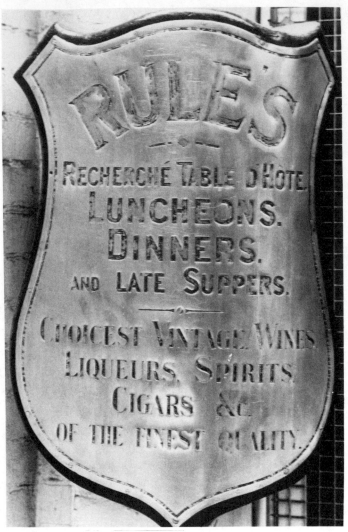

Dickensian restaurant, Maiden Lane

doorway is still there. Lillie Langtry's portrait now hangs in the alcove.

Rule's still has a fairly well-heeled clientele. Cabinet ministers sometimes dine here. The prices aren't extravagant. As well as more exotic dishes, Rule's serves roast beef and Yorkshire pudding, which makes it unusual among good London restaurants. Middle- and upper-class people in England like to eat un-English food when they dine out; beef and Yorkshire pudding are things they can always get at home. The result for foreign visitors is that these traditional English dishes are often unobtainable.

If you eat at Rule's, the staff will gladly show you the two famous alcoves. And from the street have a look at the worn brass plate by the door on the right that advertises the restaurant. Replacing it with a new one would be unthinkable; an old plate shows that you have been trading successfully for many years and is also very chic, particularly if it's been polished so much that it's almost unreadable.

Go back down Maiden Lane, passing the back of the Adelphi Theatre again, until you come to the corner on the right with **Bedford Street.** At this corner, **no. 39–40** Bedford Street, are the offices of a very British magazine, *The Lady*. Founded in Covent Garden in 1885 as *The Lady, A Journal for Gentlewomen*, it has been on its present site since 1891. A thoughtful and pleasant magazine, *The Lady* still contains interesting traces of aristocratic British society. Ladies who advertise for servants in the magazine expect their titles to be helpful. One recent advertisement read: "TITLED LADY requires full- or part-time living-in nurse companion."

There are also advertisements for nannies and governesses. *The Lady* has many articles on travel—a tradition that perhaps dates back to the days of the British Empire. Many of its readers must have been the wives and daughters of colonial administrators and businessmen, and even back in England these ladies would have kept an affectionate interest in remote and sunny lands. Today *The Lady*'s readership is largely middle class, and definitely unrebellious; but the magazine is not a cozy and uncritical journal for homemakers. Over the years it has quietly supported the rights of professional women, and now, as the magazine becomes more modern, it is losing most of its aristocratic flavor. When it expresses strong criticism, the tone is acidic rather than strident— exactly the style of genteelly educated English women. (It calls to mind the words of the discreet but formidable Florence Nightingale, who in the 1850s criticized the mountainous, self-indulgent women who were then practicing nursing. "Drunken dames of 14 stone and over must be barred," she wrote. "The provision of bedsteads is not strong enough.") To understand *The Lady* and the genteel women it addresses, you need an eye for wry humor and understatement, ways in which English ladies have traditionally made their point.

Turn right and go up Bedford Street, crossing Henrietta Street on the right, until you come to a small court, also on the right, called **Inigo Place.** This is the entrance to the churchyard of **St. Paul's Covent Garden** (not to be confused with St. Paul's Cathedral, a quite separate building about a mile to the east of here). The coat of arms, with lion and scallop shells, above the gates into Inigo Place is that of the Dukes of Bedford, who used to own the district. The churchyard is large and quiet, shut in by the backs of nineteenth-century buildings with tall, slender windows. The buildings form a windbreak, making this a fine place to rest on a sunny day. The churchyard isn't easy to spot from the road, and it is not often discovered by visitors. The locals know it, though, and in summer often come here for a picnic lunch.

In the evening the churchyard is a romantic and little-used spot, with a double line of low gas lamps running to the front of the church. By standing on one of the wooden seats, you can examine a lamp's mechanism. You will see that the pipe that carries the gas comes up through the center of the lamp standard. The lamps are crowned by models of a ducal coronet—homage, again, to the Dukes of Bedford.

The church itself is Italian in style, with a shallowly angled roof and two large bells housed in the pediment. It is a late-eighteenth-century replacement of a burned seventeenth-century original. The original was built in the same style and was a vital part of Inigo Jones's grand design for Covent Garden.

Long before the coming of the gas lamps, in 1670 this churchyard is said to have been the scene of a sinister funeral by torchlight. The dead man was Claude Duval, a Frenchman from Normandy and a highwayman, reputed to be a chivalrous robber and ladies' man. Duval was hanged at Tyburn in West London, and respected reference books say that he was buried here at St. Paul's Church with a striking poem inscribed on his gravestone:

> *Here lies Du Vall: reader, if male thou art,*
> *Look to thy purse; if female, to thy heart.*
> *Much havoc has he made of both: for all*
> *Men he made stand, and women he made fall.*
> *The second conqueror of the Norman race,*
> *Knights to his arms did yield, and ladies to his face.*
> *Old Tyburn's glory, England's illustrious thief,*
> *Du Vall the ladies' joy, Du Vall the ladies' grief.*

Glamorous highwaymen breed legends, and—as we'll see in a moment—there may be more to this poem than meets the eye. Within months of Duval's execution, a satire was published anonymously which reported a story of the highwayman's gallantry. One day Duval was robbing a coach that happened to have a young lady in it. She,

> to shew she was not afraid, takes a flageolet out of her pocket and plays. Du Vall takes the hint, plays also, and excellently well, upon a flageolet of his own. . . . Sir, says he to the person in the coach, your lady plays excellently, and I doubt not but that she dances as well, will you please to walk out of the coach, and let me have the honour to dance . . . with her upon the heath?

They danced, then Duval showed his courtesy by robbing the couple of only £100, although he knew that they had another £300 in their coach. He called the theft "paying for the music."

The satire hints strongly that Duval was bisexual, saying that in France no one of either sex could resist him, and goes on to "report" the poem in the church here. A close look at the poem shows that it makes—cleverly and discreetly—a similar point about his sexual tastes. "Knights to his arms did yield, and ladies to his face" contains a pun. "All men he made stand, and women he made fall" has a similar double meaning; the word *stand* is often used like this by risqué seventeenth- and eighteenth-century writers. If this interpretation is right, the poem was probably too erotic to have been inscribed in a church. It isn't in St. Paul's Church now, and there seems to be no serious record of anyone's ever having seen it there. I suspect it never was there: the satirist made it up for fun and has accidentally deceived local historians who haven't looked at his work carefully. (I have found a record of Duval's burial in the register of St. Giles's Church nearby, which helps to bear out this theory.)

Returning from the churchyard to Bedford Street, turn right and walk to the next corner, **King Street.** The building on the corner to your right, now a bank, was the headquarters of the British Communist Party from the 1920s to the early 1980s. The Party had a few Members of Parliament in the 1920s and late 1940s, but since then has been powerless at elections. Back in Russia, some senior Stalinist long ago complained that "our British Party will neither live nor die." The windows of the national offices here were, appropriately, made of thick opaque glass; George Orwell complained of the "dishonesty that goes on behind those thick glass windows in King Street." In his book *Spycatcher*, Peter Wright tells of his experience bugging this building for British intelligence in the late 1950s. A microphone had to be fixed into the wall, from the street. So agents of MI5 and their spouses were disguised as familiar Covent Garden types—drunken theatergoers in late evening. These all-too-sober people in their finery then crowded by the wall of the Communists' headquarters, pretending to revel. Their real purpose was to shield their technical man as he drilled into the wall and caught the telltale brick dust in his handkerchief. Wright states proudly that for months the microphone gave excellent coverage of the comrades' innermost meetings.

From Bedford Street turn left into the narrow **New**

Row (opposite King Street). Fifty yards along, at **no. 12** New Row, is a building that used to be a fruit and vegetable warehouse in the days of Covent Garden market. Today antique scientific instruments are sold here. Arthur Middleton, who owns the business, is a surveyor by training. Many of the instruments he sells were made for navigation in the nineteenth century or earlier—sextants and hand held naval telescopes.

The shop gleams with brass. The large amounts of brass used in antique instruments helped eventually to make them very scarce. During both world wars, the authorities in German-occupied Europe demanded that old instruments be given up so that the brass could be reused for armaments. The antique medical instruments sold here have proved popular with physicians, as conversation pieces or toys. I was shown a device for trepanning—drilling holes in the human skull. Devices like this were used long before anesthetics. I was also shown a jar for keeping leeches, the charming little creatures used by doctors for sucking out human blood. Doctors in England practiced bleeding their patients until the 1920s. The word *leech* came to have two meanings: the little worms themselves, and the doctors who used them. One Victorian dictionary in England said dryly, "*Leech*: a blood-sucking worm; a physician."

Running into New Row on the left here is the street called **Bedfordbury.** A few steps down, between nos. 23 and 24, you'll find an unremarkable entry labeled **Goodwin's Court.** Few Londoners notice it, so Goodwin's Court is still a superbly preserved and almost secret eighteenth-century street. Go a few steps up the entry from Bedfordbury; along the south side of the court is a row of narrow houses with bow fronts. Parts of these houses date back to the end of the seventeenth century, but bow fronts were not used until the mid-eighteenth century. Look through some of the windows; the rooms behind them are tiny. The small staircase to the next story begins in the front room because there is no back room or hall.

Walk 20 yards down the court, past the smell of curry from the kitchen of an Indian restaurant, and look back at the house built over the entry to the court.

Goodwin's Court owes a lot to its present owners, the Sympson family. When the Sympsons first moved here, around 1930, the court was a slum alley—a survivor of the old Bedfordbury hovels that Dickens mentions in *Bleak House*. Residents sat shelling peas on their door-steps. Children ran barefoot across the alley. Late at night one drunken old dame used to relieve herself simply by lifting her skirts over a grating. The court was then con-demned and slated for demolition by the local authority; its residents were mostly rehoused. But the family bravely defied the order and restored part of the court so skillfully that the row of seventeenth-century houses was allowed to remain. The two bow fronts nearest you as you enter from Bedfordbury were rebuilt; the rest are from the eighteenth century. This row of old houses is still owned, and beauti-fully maintained, by the Sympsons, who are rightly proud of what they have saved for London. At night, when the light from the Victorian gas lamps is reflected in the long line of bow windows, this quiet courtyard is perhaps one of the finest places in the city.

Look back and upwards, at the wall above the pas-sage you have just come through. Over the first window, and below the clock, is a prettily painted metal plaque about nine inches long. It shows a building in the City of London—the Royal Exchange, the headquarters of the company that once owned the sign. This is a fire mark, a badge used from the early 1700s until 1833 to show that a building was protected by a particular insurance company. At that time the only effective fire brigades were those organized by private insurance firms. The firemen in these brigades would often refuse to use their equip-ment on a burning building unless it was insured with their company. Since owners could hardly be expected to produce their insurance documents during a fire, the insurance companies insisted that their clients affix metal fire marks outside their buildings. The marks, often made by women, had many attractive designs and made good advertisements. Nowadays a fire mark on a house suggests that it had a prosperous owner 150 years ago or more. The fire marks also proved to be insurance against one's enemies. In the eighteenth century, if you didn't like someone, a fairly common way to express your animosity was to burn the person's house down. But if you saw a fire mark you might think twice. The penalties for arson were severe, and if your enemy was insured anyway, why bother?

Competition between insurance companies sometimes led to wild scenes. If a burning building had a rich owner, or was insured with more than one company, rival brigades were eager to arrive first at the fire, to collect the special reward laid down by law. Horse-drawn fire engines, painted in the companies' liveries, raced each other through the streets. The firemen sometimes brawled and slashed at each other's hoses. Company firemen were not always paid a retainer, but rather were rewarded for each fire attended. One of the attractions of serving in a company brigade was that you got legal protection from the press-gang—the government organization that virtually kidnapped men and forced them to join the navy.

If a company brigade wouldn't help at a fire, the victims had to hope that they might get a little help from the parish fire engine, which was supported with local taxes. These engines could be absurdly inefficient, as Dickens describes:

> We never saw a parish engine at a regular fire but once. It came up in gallant style—three miles and a half an hour at least. . . . Bang went the pumps, the people cheered, the beadle [a parish official] perspired profusely, but it was unfortunately discovered . . . that nobody understood the process by which the engine was filled with water, and

Goodwin's Court

that 18 boys and a man had exhausted themselves in pumping 20 minutes without producing
the slightest effect!

To see the old market and the center of Covent Garden you will need to retrace your route a few hundred
yards. I suggest going back up Goodwin's Court. Where
it ends, turn left into Bedfordbury and then right, by the
shop with the scientific instruments, into New Row. After
about 50 yards, New Row ends at the five-road intersection we saw earlier. The second exit here, working clock-
wise from your left, is narrow, quiet and paved with
flagstones—**Rose Street**; go across to it. In earlier times
this street was well known to writers. The seventeenth-
century poet Samuel Butler lived for many years, and
died, in a house here. He's best known for a poem called
"Hudibras." In 1679 the racy and highly successful playwright John Dryden was beaten up one night in Rose
Street. Despite his sizable reward of £50 for information
about who had organized the beating, he was never able
to prove publicly who the culprit was. The usual suspect
nowadays is the Earl of Rochester, who may have thought
that Dryden had attacked him in print.

Notice the curled iron lamp-support high on the front
of the **Lamb and Flag** pub. It now supports a flower
basket in summer. The inside of the building shows how
a lot of the best London pubs used to be before the mod-
ernization of the last few years. An old-fashioned strong
beer (Director's) is served by hand pump. The sparse
decor was common before brewers began trying hard to
attract female customers. A wooden beam over the bar is
decorated with a famous Medieval Latin poem in praise
of liquor:

> Meum est propositum in taberna mori;
> Vinum sit appositum morientis ori,
> Ut dicant, cum venerint, angelorum chori,
> "Deus sit propitius huic potatori."

(The sign painter has garbled the Latin, especially in the last two lines.) The poem means:

> *To die in a pub is my definite plan,*
> *With my mouth to the tap, just as close as I can.*
> *Then the angels would say, when their singing began,*
> *"O Lord, please show mercy to this boozy man."*

After the first edition of this book appeared, I was surprised to find that my translation has itself been painted up over the bar.

In the eighteenth century there was a literary gent living in Rose Street—Edmund Curll, a publisher who specialized in erotic books. Several of Covent Garden's authors survived by writing steamy stuff for Mr. Curll. Curll was persecuted by the authorities, told off by the House of Lords, imprisoned, and pilloried. (Being forced to stand in a pillory was serious punishment—you were an easy target for projectiles: litter, fruit, and dead cats.)

Come back a few yards down Rose Street, following the sharp bend to the left as it joins **King Street**, which will lead you to the Central Market and the heart of Covent Garden. Just past the bend, on the left, is **no. 27** King Street, the headquarters since 1812 of the Westminster Fire Office and its successor companies. Founded in 1717, the Westminster was one of the insurance firms that ran a private brigade of fire fighters. By crossing the street here, you can see, high on the front of the building, a very large and brightly painted molding of the Westminster's old badge. It shows a portcullis (a fortified screen for a castle gateway) crowned with three feathers. The three feathers are the traditional emblem of the Prince of Wales, the heir apparent to the throne. When the Westminster adopted them for its badge, it was with reference to the Prince of Wales who became King George II. George, who reigned from 1727 to 1760, was not one of Britain's most distinguished monarchs; his irreverent courtiers called him "Old Square-Toes." But he was one of the Westminster's earliest customers, and the company was proud to advertise that fact.

A hundred yards farther along, **no. 43** King Street is the grandest surviving eighteenth-century house in Covent Garden. It has four stories and a flat front. On the second and third stories two pilasters with elaborate capitals divide the façade into three sections. The house was built in 1716–17 for Admiral Edward Russell, Earl of Orford, a relative of the Russell family that owned Covent Garden. Russell was at that time one of the most powerful men in the country, and as Lord High Admiral had the enormous salary of £7,000 a year. He had become famous in 1692 as commander of the British fleet which defeated the French at the battle of La Hogue, off the coast of northern France; that defeat ended the hopes for a comeback of the Catholic King James II, who had lived under the protection of the French government since he had been driven from England in 1688. In Russell's great house here, the main dining room was on the first story, the master bedroom on the second, and the rooms of senior servants on the third.

Long after Russell's death, in 1856, a music hall called Evans's was built at the back of the house, and the management tried to make the place into a smart dining establishment. Music halls of the nineteenth and early twentieth centuries are remembered now in Britain as jolly places in which liquor flowed plentifully but which were—like the modern pub—generally wholesome. This image, however, is a long way from the Victorian reality; Evans's had to battle to stay decent. Female customers were not welcome; they had to give their names and addresses upon entering and were allowed to watch the performers only through a screen. These restrictions were meant to combat what Victorians called simply "the great social evil"—prostitution. From the seventeenth to the nineteenth century, Covent Garden swarmed with whores, and the music halls were one of their favorite "pitches." In at least one London music hall of the era

Gaslights and a Lord High Admiral's house, Covent Garden

the women used to do the whole of their business in the boxes. And one of the advertisements for Evans's virtually admitted that for a time whoredom had gained the upper hand here.

Opposite no. 43, fifty yards away across the flagstones, is the portico at the eastern end of **St. Paul's Church.** Like the rest of the church, it was built in the 1790s, following the earlier designs of Inigo Jones. In the Covent Garden that Jones constructed, similar colonnades were formed on the northern and eastern sides of the central rectangle, to harmonize with the portico here on the west. None of these original porticos remains, but you can see a nineteenth-century version of part of the northern portico adjoining Edward Russell's house. The open space, which made the piazza with its porticos a visible unity, has also gone, filled by the elegant Central Market of 1830.

In the church portico, notice the two gas lamps with reflectors mounted on massive iron brackets to match the grand scale of the portico itself. This spot has been a focus of Covent Garden events for centuries. In 1662, close to here, Samuel Pepys twice watched puppet shows. In the eighteenth century, Tom King's, a famous coffee-house and brothel, stood against St. Paul's portico. King himself was a renegade member of the upper class; after his death, his widow, Moll King, became famous as the manager of the place. In 1739 the law caught up with her, charged her with keeping a disorderly house, and she spent some time in prison.

Later in the century there were rather more serious disorders here. The site was used for voting in parliamentary elections, and a wooden speaker's platform was built against the portico. Voting was done in public; people shouted threats and promises at the voters, and riots often developed. In 1784 the radical Charles James Fox was elected M.P. here after a wild campaign. His female supporters promenaded the streets with little replicas of foxtails as advertisements. At that time so few people were allowed to vote that it was possible to offer handsome inducements to those who could. Among Fox's women admirers were the attractive Duchess of Devonshire and her sister. These two ladies visited wavering voters in their homes, flattering and dazzling the men with their aristocratic charm. Rumors inevitably circulated about just how far they would go in revealing the attractions of voting for Fox.

During the riots at this election several people were killed. Gangs, which included impressively physical Irish coal-heavers and sedan-chair men, were organized to protect Fox and his supporters. (Sedan-chair men practiced their trade intensively at Covent Garden, waiting in long lines in the streets to be hired by people leaving the theaters; their chairs were miniature single-person carriages supported on long poles by two men, one in front and one behind. Sedan-chair men tended to be hefty, of course, and so were useful to hire for a riot.)

In more recent times St. Paul's portico has been the setting of the opening scene of the musical *My Fair Lady* and of George Bernard Shaw's play *Pygmalion*, on which the former is based. Eliza Doolittle, a Cockney flowerseller, is trying to sell violets to wealthy people who crowd under the portico when it rains. Her accent is heard with interest by Henry Higgins, an expert on pronunciation, and he promises to convert her Cockney speech into upper-class diction within three months. In his play, Shaw, an Irishman, was satirizing English class divisions and the accents that helped to create them. He wrote in the introduction, "It is impossible for an Englishman to open his mouth without making some other Englishman hate or despise him."

Dickens, like Shaw, had fun with Cockney speech—the speech of nearly all working-class Londoners. Cockney continues to flourish today, though it has changed a little since Dickens's time. People no longer use *w* in place of *v* ("Werry good, sir") or add *h*'s in an attempt to be genteel. ("I do happreciate that.") In present-day Cockney, vowels are very different from those of BBC

English, and consonants sometimes turn into vowels or disappear. In Cockney, the sentence "Here, put that in your mouth, will you?" would sound like "Eeya, pu de i yer mahf, wi-oo ya?"

Facing the portico of St. Paul's, about 50 yards east across the flagstones, is the **Central Market** designed largely by the Georgian architect Charles Fowler. This building replaced the ramshackle collection of sheds and stalls that formed the market where the young Dickens had gazed at pineapples. For the market business, Fowler created a set of arcades running from east to west. At each end are columns and a triangular pediment, designed to match the roof and columns of St. Paul's Church. The market now has great arched roofs, added in Victorian times.

Walk over to the market's southwest pavilion—the square building at the right-hand corner as you look out from the church portico. On the wall, in faded but distinct nineteenth-century lettering, is an advertisement for one of the firms that traded here: JA'S. BUTLER, HERBALIST & SEEDSMAN, LAVENDER WATER ETC. It is said that Mr. Butler specialized in selling hedgehogs. These animals, although flea-ridden, were kept in London homes because they ate beetles and cockroaches.

For over a century, the character of Covent Garden has been dictated by what happens in the Central Market. In the mid-nineteenth century the surrounding area teemed with fruit vendors, many of them immigrants speaking Irish Gaelic. A century later, the market trade clogged the neighboring streets with trucks, and tradespeople moved into many of the fine buildings around the market. Admiral Russell's house was taken over, and a great gash was made in its front to allow trucks access to the basement. In the late 1970s, after the market trade was removed, the Central Market remained unused. For perhaps the first time since the Middle Ages, the market and Covent Garden were quiet. Then, in 1980, the building reopened as an expensive shopping mall. The wealthy patrons it has attracted have created hopes of higher profits in the whole neighborhood. Rents have risen, and some of Covent Garden's traditional businesses, such as publishing houses and specialty shops, are moving away. But creative Covent Garden is regrouping around Neal Street, only a few hundred yards to the north.

For a while in the 1970s it seemed that the Central Market might be destroyed. A group in the Greater London Council—then London's governing body—planned to demolish it and build lucrative offices in its place. Maiden Lane was also marked for destruction, to make way for a broad highway. Rule's restaurant and the gas lamps would have vanished, and Covent Garden in general would have ceased to be a pleasant place. But the plans were dropped—in the mid-1970s British property speculators ran short of money, fortunately.

Head back toward Admiral Russell's house, and turn right to pass along the Victorian portico on the northern side of the Central Market. At the first corner, with James Street, is **The Rock Garden,** a restaurant with tables out under the portico in summer, and a cellar where bands blast away in the evenings. James Street is crossed by two more roads, Floral Street (gaslit) and Long Acre. On the corner with Long Acre is Covent Garden tube station. However, I suggest not going up to James Street on this walk. Cross it instead, and continue along the side of the Central Market. At the corner where the market ends is a small patch of open ground with stone seats and some inexpensive attempts at landscape gardening. On a sunny day you might find an occasional derelict lolling here. Locally, derelicts are called "dossers"; "to doss" means "to sleep rough."

Twenty yards away, across **Russell Street** and facing the eastern end of the market, is **Tutton's,** which opened in 1977. It has become one of the most pleasant of London's moderately priced restaurants. Previously, the building was a potato warehouse for the market; the present door frames were made from warehouse floorboards.

When first constructed in 1887, the building was a hotel. You can see a faded mosaic from that era high on the wall at the end of the bar.

Perhaps without knowing it, Tutton's keeps up two local traditions. In the seventeenth century there was a Turkish bath on this site, where young men cleaned and revived themselves after an interlude in the brothels of nearby Drury Lane. The brothels have gone; they're now in Soho and Mayfair. But with the theaters and restaurants to attract revelers, there are still heavy nights to be had in Covent Garden. Breakfast at Tutton's afterwards aids a graceful recovery. In the eighteenth century, grand literary gents of Covent Garden used to hold court for hours and hours in the coffeehouses and clubs here in Russell Street. Nowadays the staff writers of the local publishing houses and advertising agencies act similarly, preening themselves a little as they sit conspicuously near the windows.

As you exit from the restaurant, you can see a long white building on your right, behind a patch of open ground: the **Royal Opera House.** Its grand entrance, with Corinthian columns, is on the side away to the right, in Bow Street. Perhaps the best-known musician to have used the Opera House is Handel, who in the 1730s had several oratorios premiered on this site. Today, the Opera House still sells some cheap tickets for its internationally renowned performances; lines of people form for hundreds of yards around the building. Many local residents stay away, thinking it mostly a place where wealthy tourists and the English upper class can glare at each other. The Opera House seems to have been rather more informal in the eighteenth and early nineteenth centuries, when audiences rioted to demand seats at prices ordinary people could afford. One price rise at that time caused "continued hissing, groaning, howling, yelling, braying, barking and hooting . . . accompanied by exclamations of 'Old Prices,' 'No Rise,' 'No Private Boxes.' " On another occasion, an increase in prices incited the audience to smash the seats and chandeliers and to rip out the linings of the boxes. Fire was an even more serious threat, destroying early versions of the Opera House. The place was largely rebuilt in 1857–58; it is this version which remains.

About 30 yards along Russell Street notice the wine bar on the left. Perhaps the most striking thing about it is its name, **Brahms and Liszt.** The name does not honor the two composers; it's an off-color Cockney joke that is used publicly only because most people don't know, or don't like to admit that they know, what it means. Cockney speech has a code of rhyming slang, sometimes said to have started as a means of communicating so that the police could not understand. "Stairs," for example, were called "apples and pears," "corner" became "Johnnie Horner" and "to pinch" (meaning "to steal") became "to half-inch." "Brahms and Liszt" is rhyming slang for "pissed" (drunk).

Twenty yards farther on, Russell Street joins Bow Street and Wellington Street. On one corner is **The Marquis of Anglesey**, one of the most popular pubs in the district because it serves the traditional hand-pumped strong beer—Real Ale, as the enthusiasts call it. The brewery that supplies the pub is Young's, an evocative name for cognoscenti of London liquor: Young's is the only brewery in the capital to have completely refused to produce draught bitter beer that is pasteurized and fizzy. Young's bitter is flat, contains living yeast, and is very strong.

Turn right at this crossroads, into **Wellington Street**. A few yards down on the right at **no. 41** is **Penhaligon's**, a perfume shop and one of the best-known specialty businesses in London. Customers have included Sir Winston Churchill and the Duke of Edinburgh. In 1975 the first story of this late-nineteenth-century building was carefully reconstructed with antique furnishings as a Victorian shop. Its perfumes and toiletries, for men and women, are all made on the premises to the recipes of

Walter Penhaligon, who founded the business in 1 Pages of his handwritten notes are displayed on the wall of the shop. On request, the perfumes are sold in antique bottles; customers can also bring their own favorite bottles to be filled.

Continue a few yards down Wellington Street, and take the first turn on the left into **Tavistock Street.** At the first corner on Tavistock Street you'll see the façade of the **Theatre Royal,** Drury Lane to the left. (Drury Lane itself runs past the back of the building.) The theater began its life in 1663, shortly after the restoration of King Charles II; the "Royal" in its title refers to him. Like the Opera House, it has twice been destroyed by fire, with the second great blaze occurring in 1809, when the playwright Richard Brinsley Sheridan was manager. The building at that time was drastically underinsured. The story goes that when Sheridan realized that the theater was well alight, he knew immediately that he was ruined and did not rush about trying to save things. Instead, he settled down with a bottle of wine at a nearby tavern to watch the blaze. When someone asked him why he wasn't making any effort to help the burning theater, he replied, "Cannot a man enjoy a glass of wine by his own fireside?"

The present building was erected in 1811–12. This is the only theater in London to have Georgian sections remaining in its interior—two grand staircases and the rotunda to which they lead. Perhaps the most pleasant part of the theater's exterior is the long colonnade on the north side. You can see it by walking a few yards up Catherine Street, past the theater entrance, and turning right into Russell Street. The colonnade was added to the building in 1831–32, early in the reign of King William IV. Its Ionic columns are of cast iron; between them, in delicate, looping brackets, are large gas lamps.

Enter the colonnade and walk about 15 yards. Here, about 14 feet up on the theater wall, you can see signs of the precautions taken when the building was new to

prevent yet another ruinous fire; next to each other, and easily missed, are two metal fire marks with initials showing that they marked the boundary between two parish fire brigades—St. Martin's and St. Paul's Covent Garden.

Perhaps the best-known person to have acted at the Theatre Royal is Nell Gwynne, a clever but illiterate woman who began her career at Drury Lane in the 1660s by selling oranges—and perhaps herself. Samuel Pepys describes happily that he kissed Nell, an ample redhead; Pepys's wife kissed her too, though no doubt with rather less enthusiasm. For a time, Pepys enjoyed hearing stories of Nell's razor tongue. But Nell came to the attention of King Charles II, who made her his mistress, and Pepys, disappointed, lost interest in her. Later, when he found himself in the box next to hers at the theater, he described sourly how "that jade Nell . . . lay there laughing upon the people."

A Protestant, Nell seems to have become popular with the London crowds, who thought of her as a rival to the King's Catholic mistress, Louise de Kéroüalle. A story is told that one day a crowd caught sight of a grand carriage with Nell inside but mistakenly assumed that it was the hated Louise. Insults flew until Nell appeared at the carriage window and called out with an actress's poise, "Pray, good people, be civil; it is the *Protestant* whore."

In England, Nell Gwynne is almost a household name. She was succeeded at the Drury Lane theater by a woman of great wit and accomplishment who is now almost entirely forgotten. This woman spent many years in Covent Garden, and the story of her wild and sad life will end this walk.

Her name was Charlotte Charke. She was born about 1710, the daughter of the highly successful actor and dramatist Colley Cibber. Interestingly, Cibber gave his daughter a liberal education; Charlotte later wrote that it "might have been sufficient for a son instead of a daughter. . . . I was never made much acquainted with a needle, which I handle with the same clumsy awkwardness a monkey does a kitten." Instead, she was taught Italian and Latin. At fourteen, she became a good shot; then a fussy woman neighbor complained that this was unfeminine. "Upon this sober lady's hint, I was deprived of my gun; and with a half-broken heart on the occasion, resolved to revenge myself, by getting a muscatoon [a type of musket] that hung over the kitchen mantelpiece, and use my utmost endeavors towards shooting down her chimneys."

Later in her teens, Charlotte used her education and social position to set herself up as a quack doctor. She afterwards admitted that she had been dreadfully ignorant of medicine. But "this defect was not discovered by my patients, as I put on significancy of countenance [a knowing air] that served to convince them of my incomparable skill and abilities." One day when she ran out of drugs she got an urgent request for medicine from an old woman. Something harmless but revolting was obviously required, to make the patient feel that it *must* be doing her good. So Charlotte collected and boiled a large number of snails, and sold the result as medicine. The old woman later returned with an eager account of the "medicine's" success, and demanded more. Charlotte noted acutely that the success of many physicians "is rather founded on the faith of the patient, than any real merit in the doctor or his prescriptions."

She married young. Her husband was a violinist, and Charlotte came to suspect that he had married her to exploit her father's influence at the Drury Lane theater. Her own motive for marrying was little better: "I thought it gave me an air of more consequence to be called Mrs. Charke than Miss Charlotte." The marriage did not last long. According to Charlotte, her husband sponged off her for money and chased after the public women of Covent Garden—"common wretches that were to be had for half a crown!" (Half a crown, incidentally, was not a trivial sum; in the 1880s prostitutes in London's rough East End were asking only a fifth of that—sixpence.)

Charlotte herself became an actress at the Drury Lane theater, and when her name first appeared in the theater's advertisements she went around London excitedly for days, gazing at them. But in 1735 she fell out with the manager at Drury Lane, a Mr. Fletewood. Feeling wronged, she retaliated by writing a play satirizing Fletewood—and herself. It was called *The Art of Management*, and seems to have been performed at least once, with Charlotte acting "herself" under the ironic (and prophetic) name of "Mrs. Tragic." Fletewood was so embarrassed that he bought up almost every printed copy of the play to prevent the public from reading it. The crumbling copy now in the library of the British Museum is one of the very few to have survived.

Charlotte's pride led to quarrels with her family. Staying with her sister once, she was given a bedroom that proved cold and leaky. She took her revenge by composing doggerel verses about the room. Criticizing the bedclothes, she wrote:

> *So charming thin, the darns so neat,*
> *With great conveniency expel the heat.*

She also quarreled with her father, who refused to see her. When she pleaded for reconciliation, he returned her letter unopened. Charlotte's revenge this time was to publish the letter—which, of course, made reconciliation even more unlikely. She denied a rumor that she had publicly slapped her father in the face with a fish. She also denied the story that, dressed as a highwaywoman with pistols, she once held up her father on the outskirts of London and robbed him of more than £60.

Charlotte seems to have been very fond of her only child, Kitty. Rejected by her family, and finding it difficult to get work as an actress, she had a hard time providing for herself and the child. At one point she tried retailing in Covent Garden: "I took it into my head to dive into TRADE. To that end, I took a shop in Long Acre, and turned oil-woman and grocer." Here she sold links for escorting coaches and sedan chairs at night. One link boy visited her shop "just before candle time, which is the dusky part of the evening, the most convenient light for perpetrating a wicked intent," and stole all her brass weights. She didn't meet him again—until one day when she caught sight of him in a cart being taken to Tyburn to be hanged.

For a time Charlotte worked as a waitress, which meant walking every night across the fields to the north-west part of Covent Garden where thieves—called foot-pads—flourished. She later wrote dryly, "I have often wondered I have escaped without wounds or blows from the gentlemen of the pad, who are numerous and frequent in their evening patrols through them fields, and my march extended as far as Long Acre, by which means I was obliged to pass through the thickest of 'em." Non-human thieves were a menace, too. Charlotte sold sausages, until a dog intervened: "Oh! DISASTROUS CHANCE! A hungry cur most savagely entered my apartment . . . and most inconsiderately devoured my remaining stock."

Faced with a grave lack of money, she was congratulated by her friends for refusing to do what innumerable women did in her position—go onto the streets. Her debts grew, and she had the terrifying experience of being put into a debtors' prison, where people could rot away for years. When released, she tried to evade her creditors by living disguised as a man. She made a good-looking man, and got an offer of marriage from an heiress. Charlotte has written wistfully about how she could have made a fortune if she had only been willing to pose as a man and marry her.

She worked for a while with a troupe of traveling actors and was briefly locked up in prison in the west of England—"among the felons, whose chains were rattling all night long, and made the most hideous noise I ever heard, there being upwards of two hundred men and boys under the different sentences of death and transportation."

In 1755 Charlotte published an autobiography; it's delightfully written in a tough, self-mocking style. She called the book "some account of my unaccountable life," and described it as "this little brat of my brain." Nearly all the above quotations are taken from it.* Though the book had some success when it first appeared (it went into two editions), it did not make Charlotte Charke's fortune. On the last occasion that we hear of this brave and talented Covent Garden character, she was growing old in poverty, with only a dog and a pet magpie for company.

*A Narrative of the Life of Mrs. Charlotte Charke, introduction by L. R. N. Ashley (Gainesville, Fla.: Scholars' Facsimiles and Reprints, 1969).

Walk · 2

Legal and Illegal London

THE INNS OF COURT

CHANCERY LANE

HOLBORN

HIGH HOLBORN

HOLBORN

Stone Bldgs.

Soane Museum

CHANCERY LANE

HOLBORN

REMNANT ST.

LINCOLN'S INN FIELDS

NEW SQ.

SERLE ST.

STAR YD.

Lincoln's Inn

Royal College of Surgeons

Record Office

PORTUGAL ST.

CAREY ST.

BELL YD.

INNER TEMPLE LN.

FLEET ST.

KINGSWAY

Temple Church

MIDDLE TEMPLE

BOUVERIE ST.

Law Courts

DEVEREUX CT.

The Temple

TEMPLE AVE.

ESSEX ST.

A L D W Y C H

STRAND

FOUNTAIN CT.

TEMPLE LA.

KING'S BENCH WK.

THE

ALDWYCH

King's College

Somerset House

TEMPLE PL.

TEMPLE

EMBANKMENT

River Thames

VICTORIA

WATERLOO BRIDGE

WALK 2: The Inns of Court

Starting Point: Holborn tube station
Buses: 8, 19, 22, 25, 38, 55, 68, 77, 77a, 77c, 170, 172, 188, 239, 501

This walk will take in three of the four Inns of Court: Lincoln's Inn, the Inner Temple, and the Middle Temple. This is perhaps the prettiest and most historical of our walks, with fewer pubs and shops than in other parts of London. One note of warning: Lincoln's Inn doesn't allow visitors on weekends. So this is a walk best done on a weekday.

The Inns of Court were formed in the Middle Ages, and were called Inns because they gave lodging to lawyers, legal students, and others in search of smart company. Until the eighteenth century, the Inns were like universities of law; sometimes there were student disturbances of a colorful and still-familiar kind. Today, with their quiet courtyards, and chambers arranged around open staircases, the Inns feel very much like Oxford or Cambridge colleges. The Inns are in the middle of town, near the boundary between the ancient cities of London and Westminster, and about half a mile east of Covent Garden. (The fourth Inn, Gray's, not on today's route, is nearby.) Their rows of fine seventeenth- and eighteenth-century buildings are fairly well hidden from the outside. People who have lived in London for years often say, when shown the Inns, that they never realized they were there.

Today the Inns are not the main centers of legal education, and students no longer live in them. The chambers in the Inns have become extremely valuable; the rent is far beyond the means of most students. They are occupied mostly by practicing barristers and solicitors—the two kinds of English lawyer. (In outline, barristers have traditionally done the professional pleading in the higher courts: solicitors do the primary research into legal cases and then instruct, or "brief," barristers to represent clients in court.)

The Inns are controlled by barristers, the more glamorous kind of lawyer. In court a barrister still wears a long black gown and a gray wig. A person in this austere costume, delivering a speech of well-rehearsed aggression, is a dramatic sight in a paneled courtroom—as barristers themselves are well aware. The main English civil courts are close to the route of our walk, and if you go through the Inns on a day in legal term (the main legal vacation occurs in August and September), you'll probably see barristers in their grand dress, walking between their chambers and the courts.

Although the Inns are now used mainly for lawyers' offices, legal students still come here when qualifying as barristers. Only by being affiliated with one of the four Inns of Court, and by passing exams set jointly by them, can a person become a barrister. Each Inn insists that its students attend a number of dinners in its hall. "Eating dinners," in the lawyers' phrase, is a student's introduction to the legal community, and this is done partly to preserve tradition and to foster camaraderie. Clients sometimes find this professional solidarity rather chilling, but the lawyers usually have more in common with one another than with the clients, and are anxious not to quarrel with their colleagues.

Each Inn is an independent body, governed by a group of its judges and senior barristers who are called Benchers (strictly, Masters of the Bench); this group serves under an annually elected official, the Treasurer. Quarrels sometimes occur between the Inns. In 1882 there was a splendidly petty wrangle when the Treasurers of the four Inns decided to send a joint declaration of loyalty to Queen Victoria. The plan almost fell through because the Treasurers disagreed as to whose signature was to appear first on the declaration. Eventually they compromised; the document was presented not by the Treasurers but by the Queen's son, Prince Edward, acting for the Inns. Even so, local chauvinism remained: a historian of the Middle Temple noted slyly that Edward was "himself a member of *our* Bench."

On the way to the Inns you will walk through Lincoln's Inn Fields, now a park set with towering plane trees but once the site of some of England's most sensational executions. The grand buildings around the Fields have some sinister tales of their own; perhaps most tragic of all, as we shall see at the end of the walk, is the story of the medieval Templar knights, who have given their name to the site of the Inner and the Middle Temple.

At the chief exit from Holborn tube station, turn left onto the main road, Kingsway. From Kingsway, take the third little entrance on the left, Remnant Street. Where Remnant Street ends, about 60 yards away, turn right and see **Lincoln's Inn Fields.** Pass along the Fields for a few yards, keeping them on your left and the row of grand houses on your right.

The sixth of these houses, **nos. 59–60,** was once among the most fashionable in London. It was built about 1640, possibly by the best-known architect of the time, Inigo Jones. Behind the tall windows on the second story were the finest rooms. The pilasters (inset columns) ris-

2

ing between the windows gave the building the desired
Italian appearance; look carefully and you will see that
they narrow toward the top. The architectural term for
this is *entasis*; it was used for the columns of Greek tem-
ples, including the Parthenon, because perfectly straight
columns gave an optical illusion of splaying at the top
and could make a building appear squat.

This house has had some noted occupants. In 1664
it was bought by an eccentric Protestant aristocrat, Charles
Powlett, who lived here for over twenty years. Powlett
was Marquis of Winchester in 1685, when a Catholic
king, James II, came to the throne; to avoid the dangerous
choice between supporting and opposing the King, he
pretended to be mad. He drove around the country
with a procession of coaches and a huge troop of horse-
men, sleeping during the daytime and giving wild parties
at night. Luckily for his finances, this act became unnec-
essary after three years, when James II was deposed.
Powlett got his reward from the incoming Protestant
rulers, William III and his wife, Mary: he was promoted
to Duke.

In 1683 Powlett's house had been used for a grisly
purpose—fitting together the body and severed head of
Lord William Russell, another Protestant, who had just
been executed for high treason in Lincoln's Inn Fields.
Russell was believed to have been plotting to kill King
Charles II and his Catholic brother, James, for fear that
James would shortly come to the throne. Powlett probably sympathized with his unlucky fellow aristocrat and
offered his house for this preliminary to burial. Later,
William and Mary tried to compensate Russell's family
by making his father, the Earl of Bedford, a duke. (The
Earl owned Covent Garden, so this was how the landlords of that area became dukes.)

In 1700 another colorful nobleman lived in this
house: Charles Sackville, Earl of Dorset. Earlier in his life
Sackville had been involved in indecent exposure, robbery, and murder. Samuel Pepys mentions in his diary

that Sackville fought and was imprisoned after "running up and down all the night almost naked through the streets." Sackville was also the lover of Nell Gwynne before she became famous as the mistress of Charles II. Later Nell is said to have called Charles Sackville "my Charles the First." At the time, he was not yet Earl of Dorset but had the title Lord Buckhurst. Pepys notes that Nell was insulted one day by a rival actress, Beck Marshall, who called her "Lord Buckhurst's whore." Nell replied that she was only one man's whore, although she had been brought up in a brothel; Beck, she said, had been brought up the daughter of a pious chapel-goer but she was now the whore of several!

Sackville was followed by yet another aristocrat, Robert Bertie, 4th Earl of Lindsey, from whom the building gets its present name, Lindsey House. In 1791 the house got its most famous resident of all. By looking through the railings outside the house, you can see a plaque to the right of the entrance dedicated to him: Spencer Perceval, the only British Prime Minister to have been assassinated.

Perceval was the second son of an earl; inheriting less than he desired, he became a barrister and also found a sinecure—such posts flourished around 1800. Perceval's sinecure was at the Royal Mint; he was "surveyor of the meltings and clerk of the irons," and the income helped him to afford Lindsey House. In 1792 Perceval was employed by the government to prosecute Tom Paine, the radical supporter of the American and French revolutions and author of *Common Sense* and *The Rights of Man*. By 1803, while still living here, Perceval was Attorney General and the prosecutor of another famous radical, Colonel Despard. Despard, unlike Paine, was actually in the hands of the government when tried, and his prosecution caused a sensation.

Despard was an Irishman with a good war record. But after his success at soldiering, he had been disappointed with his treatment by the government and had turned to radicalism. In 1802 he was charged with plotting to kill the King, the frequently insane George III. A witness called by Perceval said that Despard had suggested firing a cannon at the King as he traveled in a coach to Parliament. The prosecution was successful; the jury voted "guilty" but strongly recommended mercy for the distinguished ex-soldier. The judge had other ideas. At the time, the rich in Britain were terrified that the French Revolution would cross the Channel. Radicals were making jokes about chopping up the nobility and turning them into "aristocrat pies." Despard, said the judge, had proposed "instead of the ancient limited monarchy of this realm . . . its useful gradations of rank, its natural and inevitable, as well as desirable inequalities of property, to substitute a wild scheme of impracticable equality"—the *égalité* of the French Revolution. Despard and associates were sentenced to hang.

With a rope around his neck, Despard was allowed to make a short speech from the scaffold to the crowd of onlookers, though he was warned that the trap would be dropped the moment he said "an inflammatory or improper word." After he had spoken briefly about despotism and his being a friend of the poor, he was stopped, and the execution took place. Two of those hanged with him didn't die quickly enough; the executioner had to tug at their legs to speed things up.

After this success in prosecuting Despard, Spencer Perceval lived for another nine years. To his credit, he did help reduce the evils of the slave trade, and he refused to prosecute the early organizers of British labor unions. In 1808 he moved from the house in Lincoln's Inn Fields to one on Downing Street. The next year he became Prime Minister. On May 11, 1812, a failed businessman named John Bellingham, with a grievance against the government, waited for Perceval in the House of Commons and shot him in the chest with a pistol. Perceval died. Bellingham was hanged a week later.

Before leaving this old house, look at the three rusting iron brackets above the railings at the front. They date from the days before gas lighting, from the eighteenth century. Inside the brackets were globes of glass, each containing an oil lamp with reservoir and wick; below each bracket is a short horizontal bar, where the lamplighter rested his ladder. In the eighteenth century, the unlit fields across the road were alive with criminals at night, and the residents of the great houses hoped that such oil lights would keep them away.

John Gay, a poet of the 1720s, knew these fields well and wrote verses advising travelers how to avoid being robbed here. They should stick to the oil-lit streets, he said, and not be tempted to hire a link man to escort them with blazing torch across the fields. Link men deliberately led travelers into ambushes and then took a share of the spoils:

> *Where Lincoln's Inn, wide space, is railed around,*
> *Cross not with venturous step; there'oft is found*
> *The lurking thief . . .*
> *Though thou art tempted by the link-man's call,*
> *Yet trust him not along the lonely wall;*
> *In the mid way he'll quench the flaming brand,*
> *And share the booty with the pilfering band.*
> *Still keep the public streets, where oily rays,*
> *Shot from the crystal lamp, o'erspread the ways . . .*

Next door is another grand residence, **nos. 57–58** Lincoln's Inn Fields. It was built in 1730 to harmonize with Lindsey House and has similar pilasters and tall windows. For most of this century the place has housed a firm of solicitors, Marks and Clerk; you can see their worn brass plate on an inner door. In front is a yard of pleasant flagstones, empty on weekends and open to the road, but I don't advise walking onto it. Once when I did, an angry gentleman told me about legal rights, saying

"How would you like trespassers in *your* back garden?" This isn't a back garden, of course, and legal rights may be different from moral rights. But on weekdays it may be best to view the house from the road.

In the mid-1780s, this was the town house of a well-known lawyer, Lord Chief Justice Mansfield. In the previous decade Mansfield had lived a little northwest of here, in Bloomsbury, but his house there had been burned down in 1780 by a rioting Protestant crowd, angry at his liberal policy toward Catholics. (More later about these rioters, many of whom were eventually shot.) Mansfield found his house in Lincoln's Inn Fields a more peaceful place. In 1788 he retired from here to Kenwood House, a mansion in Hampstead.

In the 1790s, the building here was divided: the graceful porch with its classical columns was installed by a leading architect, John Soane, in an attempt to distract attention from the new and demeaning double doors. The section on the right, no. 58, became well known to Charles Dickens, because from 1834 to 1856 this was the home of his friend and biographer John Forster. Dickens mentions the place in *Bleak House*, imagining it as the home of the secretive lawyer Tulkinghorn, whose eventual murder in the house is described with satisfaction.

On December 2, 1844, Dickens came to no. 58 to give a private reading of "The Chimes," a tearful story about the poor. One of the people in his small audience did a satirical drawing of the occasion: it shows two of the male listeners apparently weeping; the host, Forster, sitting apelike in the foreground; and the divine Dickens reading with a supernatural light radiating from his head.

The reading was such a success that he was persuaded to repeat the performance three days later. These may have been Dickens's first dramatic readings from his work; years later, similar readings to large audiences were to kill him. There was a huge demand for such readings;

by his late forties Dickens was desperately overworked, and his portraits show a ravaged, weary face. He was already wealthy but remained anxious for money. In deciding to give a tour of readings in the United States when he was in his mid-fifties, he admitted that the "likelihood of making a very great addition to my capital in half a year" was "an immense consideration." He made nearly £20,000 (a huge amount in those days) in America. In New York people spent large sums simply to buy places in line for the readings. Back in England, Dickens, against medical advice, took on even more readings, collapsed, and died.

Cross the road directly opposite no. 58, and take the path into the park, **Lincoln's Inn Fields** proper. One hundred yards' walk will bring you to the park's center, a space canopied by plane trees surrounding a wooden pavilion. Marked out in the shade here are two netball courts, used at lunchtime by young women from the nearby offices. Netball is rather like basketball, and in Britain is played almost exclusively by women; but the spectators who gather here at midday to watch the short-skirted players are almost all men.

The outer fields are much used in summer for eating, sunbathing, and courting. In earlier times they were less attractive. In 1735 an Act of Parliament reported that "the great square . . . Lincoln's Inn Fields . . . hath for some years past lain waste and in great disorder, whereby the same has become a receptacle for rubbish, dirt and nastiness of all sorts." The Act went on about "robberies, assaults, outrages and enormities" which happened here. One incident in the 1730s involved a senior legal official, Sir Joseph Jekyll, who had promoted a law which put a tax on liquor of £1 per gallon; drinkers retaliated by beating him up in Lincoln's Inn Fields. The government then had to provide Jekyll with a guard of sixty soldiers. His law was known as the "gin act," gin (mixed with fruit juice) being the great opiate of the eighteenth-century English masses. William Hogarth, an artist of the time,

produced famous paintings of the horrors of gin drinking; some of his original work can now be seen in Lincoln's Inn Fields at the Soane Museum. (Though the
museum isn't part of the walk today, you could reach it
by turning left at the wooden pavilion, and leaving the
park by the path which then faces you. The museum
specializes in interior furnishings, and is at no. 13, Lincoln's Inn Fields.)

The grim fields were a suitable place for well-attended
executions. In 1586, fourteen men were convicted of
plotting to kill Protestant Elizabeth I, and of attempting
to put on the throne her Catholic cousin, Mary Queen of
Scots. They were executed here, some of them by a bar-
baric procedure—hanging, drawing, and quartering—
which meant being hanged for a short time, castrated,
disemboweled while alive, chopped into quarters, and
beheaded. Quartering allowed parts of the victim to be
publicly displayed in several places, a warning to as many
subjects as possible of the dangers of plotting against the
sovereign. Great care was taken with the quarters and
severed heads; after the execution they were boiled in
the hangman's cauldron to preserve them and to make
them less palatable to birds.

One of the plotters in 1586, Anthony Babington,
showed a striking composure during the execution here.
His fellow convicts knelt in prayer, but Babington stood
with his hat on and calmly watched the executioner's
knife do to the first victim what it was shortly to do to
him. Mary Queen of Scots had written earlier to encourage Babington in his plot, and it was this which gave
Queen Elizabeth's government its public justification for
beheading Mary herself in the following year.

Turn right at the pavilion, and the path will take you
out of the park to a spot where you will encounter a vast
classical structure. This is the façade of the **Royal College
of Surgeons**—pompous, and probably meant to be. The
college sets examinations in surgery; lectures and exper-
iments are also held here. Today surgeons in England

have, of course, a flawless reputation (save for the occasional one who mistakenly sews up an instrument inside a living patient). But this good name has not always existed. In the early nineteenth century surgeons performed grim and clumsy operations, and sometimes had characters to match. Needing fresh corpses to dissect, some surgeons of the time were notorious for their links with the "resurrectionists"—men who illegally dug up the dead for sale as medical specimens. When, in the 1840s, Florence Nightingale told her grand and wealthy parents that she wished to practice nursing, they could not at first understand. The nurses of the day were, as one authority put it, "without exception drunkards." At last her mother thought she had the explanation: Florence must be in love "with a low, vulgar surgeon."

The surgeons' impressive building here, mostly built in the 1830s, was designed by a fashionable architect, Charles Barry (he also designed the present Houses of Parliament). Barry was almost certainly trying to improve the surgeons' unfortunate image by making them a splendid and dignified headquarters. Notice the vast columns at the front, surmounted by ramshorn curls ("Ionic volutes," in architects' jargon). Horrifying medical practices went on for some time after the 1830s. John Hall, a senior military physician during the Crimean War of the 1850s, refused to let his surgeons use the new anesthetic, chloroform. Instead, amputations had to be carried out on fully conscious patients, sometimes by moonlight. Charles Barry's vast building stands as an overwhelming tomb, a memorial to the bad old days of English surgery.

As you leave the park, turn left onto the sidewalk, and 100 yards ahead you will see a large, arched gateway. Go through it (unless it's Saturday or Sunday), and you are inside **Lincoln's Inn.**

The Inn has been here since before 1422; its surviving records begin in that year, but the place had obviously been flourishing earlier. The name Lincoln is rather mysterious; it may have come from a medieval Earl of

NO PARKING
ON PAVEMENT
UNDER ANY
CIRCUMSTANCES

LINCOLN'S INN
VISITORS
CAR PARK

TWO HOURS
OR PART OF   50p

A FURTHER
CHARGE OF   £1.00

WILL BE MADE FOR ANY
SUBSEQUENT PERIOD OF
ONE HOUR
OR PART THEREOF

Lincoln who had a house nearby. The oldest building to be seen nowadays is the Old Hall, built in 1489 of red brick; you can see it from the entrance, 100 yards straight ahead between the trees. You'll reach it in a few minutes; first, though, go 10 yards inside the entrance and look left at the hefty door set in the wall and studded with iron. This is part of a Victorian upstairs-downstairs arrangement. The door leads to a steep flight of steps which descend to the kitchens of the Inn. Look up and you will see the end of the hall where the lawyers dine—upstairs. The architecture of the hall resembles that of around 1600. You will see the building from a better angle in a moment, but from here you can see its true date, 1843, confessed in blue brick above the great window. Also in blue brick are the initials of the architect: P. H. (Philip Hardwick).

Go 20 yards beyond the kitchen doorway, and turn left up the first flight of steps. Where these steps themselves turn left you'll see an ornamented water tank made of lead. In summer it is overhung by flowering fuchsias; part these, and see the date molded into the metal: 1685. (There will be something to say later about this eventful year, in which Charles II died and was succeeded, with much bloodshed, by his brother James.) The steps here lead to the entrance of the hall, and have metal fixtures for carpet rods. Since the steps are outdoors, a carpet can be laid only on rare occasions, such as a royal visit.

At the top of the steps on the left you get a good view of the hall where trainee barristers "eat their dinners" in the company of their seniors. Notice the intricate decoration in the imitation-Tudor design on the tall chimney pots and the two-storied cupola on the roof, equipped with its own miniature flying buttresses.

Go along the gravel to the far end of the hall, where the library of the Inn juts out at a right angle. Just to the left of the library steps is another antique water tank; the design shows cherubs pulling a chariot. High on the library wall, to the right of the steps, is a coat of arms with an appropriate legal motto in rhyming Latin: *Pro rege, lege, grege*— "On behalf of the king, the law, and the herd," in that order.

Go down the steps on the right, and a few yards ahead of you will be a little nineteenth-century hut built of brick. Ten feet tall and 7 feet wide, it is crowned by pinnacles and has a pointed Gothic arch over the door. It is used to store garden tools, and has been called the "**Head Gardener's Castle.**" The architect, George Gilbert Scott, also built the large and serious set of legal chambers behind it. He was, to put it mildly, a Gothic enthusiast, and even the little hut needed its formal Gothic decoration. I was told that earlier in this century the hut was used as a den by an eminent lawyer. It seems to have been designed originally for the servant who looked after the horses and carriages of visitors. Outside the hut the drive widens into a large rectangle: here the servant turned the carriages around, to be ready for departure.

Just beyond the Gardener's Castle is the start of a long stone eighteenth-century building. Two-thirds of the way along its façade is a fine sundial, decorated in blue and gold. For a better view of it, go a few yards up the path that winds away to the left into the garden of the Inn. The inscription on the sundial reads:

T
Rt. Hon.
W. P.
1794

The large "T" stands for Treasurer of the Inn; "Rt. Hon." (Right Honourable) means that the Treasurer commemorated here was a member of the Privy Council, a senior body of state; "W. P." are his initials—William Pitt, who was at the time Prime Minister.

Pitt was in several ways a striking man. He had become Prime Minister at the age of twenty-four—his father had been Prime Minister, which helped. When the news of the young Pitt's appointment was given to the House of Commons, it was met with a howl of laughter. As Prime Minister, Pitt opposed the revolutionary French overseas, and tried to crush radicals at home who sympathized with France. The radicals retaliated with abuse and satire. It was pointed out that Pitt spent curiously little time with women; as one wit naughtily put it, referring to Britain personified as the lady Britannia, Pitt wasn't fit to stand at Britannia's head if he couldn't stand at her tail. Pitt was, however, tempted by liquor, especially port. He entered the House of Commons one day dead drunk, with his friend Henry (Hal) Dundas, who was in a similar state—too drunk, perhaps, to make out the Speaker of the House. The incident became famous; an eminent scholar of the time wrote a parody:

> PITT: I can't discern the Speaker, Hal; can you?
> DUNDAS: Not see the Speaker! Damn me, I see two.

Pitt died at forty-six after an effective career as a Conservative. Parliament arranged to pay his debts of £40,000.

Several other British Prime Ministers have qualified as barristers at Lincoln's Inn, including the great nineteenth-century rivals, Disraeli and Gladstone. (It was Disraeli who shrewdly bought a large British holding in the Suez Canal Company, highly profitable before 1956.) In the early 1950s Mrs. Margaret Hilda Thatcher "ate dinners" here, after some years as a research chemist.

At the far end of the lawn facing Pitt's sundial you may see, in summer, metal hoops set up for the gentle and skilled game of croquet. At lunchtime the public is allowed to go right along the path by this lawn. When you walk back, keep the Gardener's Castle on your left and the mock-Tudor hall on your right; on reaching the road that runs from the main entrance of the Inn, turn

left and walk the 50 yards to the place where the chapel and Old Hall join. The **chapel,** on the left, has been largely rebuilt in this century; it was one of the few London buildings to be bombed in the First World War. (The bombing at that time caused such panic that in the 1930s many expected London's morale to collapse within days if there were ever to be a second war with Germany.) The previous chapel was built in the 1620s on stone piers, which are still standing; go through the chapel entrance; and walk in the undercroft between the piers. This cold but dry space underneath the chapel once served as a rendezvous. Samuel Pepys mentions meeting an acquaintance here in 1663. Set in the floor are gravestones, many of them made unreadable through wear. Go to the central pier; two feet from it, to the left, you can still make out the name on the gravestone of John Thurloe, secretary of state in the 1650s, during the short era when England was a republic. As the assistant of Oliver Cromwell, Thurloe ran a superb spy network which penetrated the court of the exiled Charles II. After Cromwell's death and Charles's return to England, Thurloe may have expected to be executed, as other prominent republicans were. But he was spared, perhaps because, as a spymaster, he knew too much about some of the King's Cavalier supporters who had been playing a double game. (Thurloe is supposed to have said that, if he were hanged, he had a "black book" which would hang many who now claimed to be loyal Cavaliers.) Thurloe retired from politics in 1660; within a few years even royalists were complaining publicly that the nation's spies weren't nearly as efficient as they had been during the republic under Thurloe's management.

Leave the undercroft by its open right side, and you'll come into a delightful little gaslit court. The brick building to your right, adjoining the chapel, is the **Old Hall,** the fifteenth-century structure which you saw earlier from a distance. From 1737 to 1875 this was where the High Court of Chancery met outside legal term. The High Court heard some of the most important disputes over property, and Dickens opened *Bleak House* in this setting. Dickens disliked lawyers; he may have considered them fellows of the legal men who had helped to imprison his own father for debt in the 1820s and 1830s. In *Bleak House* he tried to convey how dismal the High Court was:

> London. Michaelmas Term lately over. . . . Implacable November weather. . . . Fog everywhere. Fog up the river . . . fog down the river. . . . And hard by Temple Bar, in Lincoln's Inn Hall, at the very heart of the fog, sits the Lord High Chancellor in his High Court of Chancery. . . .

The fog symbolizes the obscurity of the law; all through the novel the property dispute of *Jarndyce* v. *Jarndyce* drags on. By the time the case is solved, no property is left—the whole estate has been used in paying lawyers' bills. Dickens based the Jarndyce affair on a real legal case; he was attacking "Chancery abuses and delays." Even today, costs in the reformed High Court can be vast. In 1990 the cost of a libel hearing, to be paid by the losing side, was over £10,000 a day—and some libel cases last for weeks. Although Chancery cases are no longer heard within Lincoln's Inn, the lawyers here still specialize in work of this kind; criminal lawyers are more likely to be found in the other three Inns.

Walk through the covered passage between the chapel and the Old Hall, noticing the timber set into the brickwork. Ahead of you and to the left is now the **garden of New Square,** overlooked on three sides by late-seventeenth-century buildings. The intricate iron gates which led into the garden are still in place, close to the road leading to the Inn's entrance; they bear the date 1863. Until the Second World War the gates were connected with iron railings around the garden, but now most of the railings have gone and the locks of the gates, unused, have largely rusted away. During the war, ornamental iron railings like these were cut down by government order. Officially, the commandeered metal was to be reused for making weapons. But rumors circulated that many railings passed the war peacefully in huge unused dumps, and that the main effect of requisitioning them had been to give the impression that the government was doing something useful.

The gardens of Lincoln's Inn now stretch from New Square up past the Gardener's Castle to the stone building, several hundred yards away. In the Middle Ages part of the gardens (the section which now faces Pitt's sundial) was called the Coneygarth, the rabbit garden. The rabbits made a good target for hungry or clowning legal students, and the Inn had to make a rule forbidding the young gentlemen to shoot arrows at them. In 1489, the time when the Old Hall was built, the Benchers of the Inn also set a fine (twenty shillings) for any member caught fornicating in the Coneygarth. No doubt because detection was far more difficult, the fine for being discovered fornicating in one's chamber at the Inn was five times as great.

After looking at the gates, turn left and go back a few yards to the first staircase entrance which faces the garden of New Square; it is marked **no. 12**. At the entrance are the names of the barristers who work here. Practicing barristers come mostly from the English upper classes, and the names on these staircases give some interesting insights into the naming habits of grand English people. At no. 12 you may see names with three initials, often a mark of pride in ancestry, suggesting that one has several forebears who deserve commemorating. You will also find compound surnames on many staircases; these are called "double-barrelled" names in England and are virtually unknown among the working class. They often originated with a marriage between two propertied families, or when a grand person became dissatisfied with being plain Smith or Jones. It is also thought rather splendid to have a *de* or *le* before one's surname; it isn't very chic in England to *be* French, but it is chic to be English with a hint of French ancestry. This feeling goes back to the Middle Ages, when the ruling class in England was of Norman-French descent.

Barristers remain a posh group partly because of the structure of the profession. Young barristers are not allowed simply to set up new practices (called "chambers") of their own; they must join one of the established chambers. And when established barristers decide whom to admit to their chambers, they frequently favor people from their own social background. If a young lawyer succeeds in the fierce competition for a place in chambers, he or she must expect, because of inexperience, to be given little work and to make little or no money for a year or two. The rent and expenses of the chambers, however, are high: the result of beginning one's career in chambers may be no net income at all, or even debt. This arrangement tends to exclude those without family money behind them. Young lawyers without inherited wealth usually become solicitors rather than barristers.

After passing nos. 12 and 13, notice the little grassy courtyard behind railings on the left, and the fine old bow window in the corner. Where the railings end, turn left into the alley; a few yards along, look up and you'll see—about eight feet above you—an inscription on the wall from 1693, a time when not all of this area belonged to Lincoln's Inn: "This wall is built upon the ground of Lincolnes Inne. No windowes are to be brocken out without leave."

Go back down the alley into New Square, and turn left. On staircase no. 1, you will see the name of a firm of solicitors. Over most of England and Wales solicitors are far more numerous than barristers, and their job seems to the public rather less exciting. Much of their work, such as drawing up wills and arranging the sale of

Barristers, Carey Street

real estate, doesn't involve action in the courts. In the relatively humble magistrates' and county courts a solicitor may act in place of a barrister, speaking and cross-questioning on behalf of a client. Some solicitors would like the right to do this in the higher courts as well; barristers, however, defend their near-monopoly by saying that solicitors are not trained in pleading and interrogation, or in the rather stagey techniques by which a barrister sometimes impresses a jury.

Right ahead of you, between staircases 3 and 4, is an arched passage leading out of New Square. On either side of the passage (officially, **Lincoln's Inn Archway**, Carey Street, London WC2) is **Wildy's,** established here in 1830, one of the best secondhand legal bookshops in the country. The staff is kind and knowledgeable.

In the windows on the left of the passage Wildy's keeps permanently on show two colorful cartoons which pleasantly satirize the legal industry. One is by H. M. Bateman, an artist who specialized in depicting social blunders—like someone in a concert audience clapping between the movements of a symphony. The cartoon here is called "The Spoilsport," or "The culprit who admitted everything," and shows a cheerful defendant ending his trial on its opening day by telling a horrified court that he is guilty. The judge tries to silence him, while rows of lawyers stare aghast at the prospect of losing a long and juicy case. The other cartoon shows two farmers in a dispute over a cow. One pulls its tail and the other its horns. Between them sits a barrister, in wig and gown, milking it. I asked at Wildy's whether the people who buy these cartoons are lawyers, and was told "Oh yes, nearly always—especially American lawyers. English lawyers perhaps find them rather near the bone."

Contrary to popular belief, barristers' earnings are often low by professional standards. There are about five thousand practicing barristers in England and Wales (Scotland has its own legal system); recently their organization, the Bar Council, complained that at least a third were earning "a pittance." An English barrister would be lucky, after taking a university degree and having five years' legal practice, to earn as much as an intelligent secretary with no legal qualifications working for the U.S. Supreme Court. English fees can be so low that even the barristers' austere set of rules sometimes relents. Very occasionally a defendant finds himself unrepresented in court and is allowed to choose any barrister present to represent him. The fee for this work, called "dock defence," is token. Most barristers eagerly avoid it, and evasive measures are permitted. As a legal textbook puts it, "There is no objection to a barrister leaving the court on hearing the prisoner ask for a dock defence, but he should not remove his wig and remain in court." Snatching off one's wig is not allowed, but running for the door is fine.

At the far end of Wildy's passage, look up at the large gaslight, which still functions. Go a few steps toward the road, then look back; in the lawyers' windows above the passage you can often see bundles of papers tied up with legal red tape (literally).

Turn right on leaving the passage, into **Carey Street.** "To be in Carey Street" is a phrase in England meaning "to be bankrupt." The grand set of buildings facing you, opened in 1882, is called the Law Courts (officially, The Royal Courts of Justice), the main group of civil courts in the country. The bankruptcy court is part of this complex. More about the Law Courts in a moment. First, though, have a look at the lawyers' pub, **The Seven Stars,** 50 yards along Carey Street on the right. Best viewed from the far side of the road, the building has been here since (it's claimed) 1602. Its two-storied frontage leans out slightly into the street, looking tiny against the backs of the Lincoln's Inn buildings that rise behind it. On the wall of the second story is a metal fire mark, prettily painted, from around 1800. It shows clasped hands and was put up by an insurance company called the Amicable Contributors.

Inside the pub are some large and prized antique mirrors, advertising forgotten brews of beer. The low ceilings bulge slightly. On the walls are old prints of noted lawyers and of characters from the novels of Dickens. The staff I met seemed frightened to talk about the place. The brewers who own most of Britain's pubs like to install managers without security of tenure. Tenants (who do have security) and owner-managers usually have more confidence and more pride in the places they run. It is sad when the management of a fine pub like this feels that all questions about it have to be referred to the public relations department of a large brewing corporation.

The **Law Courts** here are built in a lofty Victorian Gothic style, with pinnacles and pointed windows, and faced in stone with bands of red brick. The stone corridors inside seem designed to resemble a medieval castle, and when I walked through them during a rainstorm they were leaking like one. For much of the year the court buildings are closed or almost empty, so I haven't routed the walk through them. If you do go in, you will find an entrance 20 yards beyond The Seven Stars. Remember that these are mainly civil courts. The Old Bailey, the Central Criminal Court, is about half a mile away to the east; that's the place for watching the big names of the criminal world—hit men, domestic murderers, and disgraced politicians. Many of the cases here are commercial. When occupied, each courtroom has a list of its cases posted outside. If you plan to stay for a good while, sit in almost any courtroom; otherwise, peep in through the glass in the court's antechamber. Even if they see you, the judges will pretend not to notice. And you do have a right to be there.

In the corridors you may see barristers talking with their clients. There's some discreet drama going on here. The barristers often look very tall with their long gowns and their upright bearing. As a barrister tilts his head back slightly, to look down at a client, the unspoken

message is that the client is really rather lucky to be represented by such a grand person. Stagey behavior isn't restricted to the courtroom.

Back in Carey Street, retrace your route, and after passing Wildy's entrance you will see a fine house (no. 60) with wooden shutters on the first story and a fanlight above the door. Immediately after this house turn left into **Star Yard**. Twenty yards up here, on the right, is the legal wig-making department of the firm **Ede and Ravenscroft**. A barrister's wig is displayed in the window. The wigs are expensive; the small wig with pigtails used by barristers costs well over £200. (The same design is used for men and women.) The long full-bottomed wigs used by judges on ceremonial occasions cost almost four times as much and take over two years to make. All the wigs are made of South American horsehair and are meant to last a lifetime. Because of the cost of purchase, judges and barristers commonly borrow wigs from one another.

The wearing of legal wigs has lasted from the seventeenth century; law is a conservative profession dominated by the elderly. It is sometimes argued that the uniform of wig and gown distracts attention from the individuality of the lawyer, helping him or her to appear almost as a personification of the law. The uniform may also persuade the public that barristers are rather majestic people, and that a client is getting good value!

Thirty yards farther up Star Yard is a rare sight in England, a tiny street urinal, made of decorative ironwork. It stands against a back wall of Lincoln's Inn. It's for men only. Notice the royal coats of arms on it, and the iron latticework at the top.

Go back down Star Yard, cross Carey Street, and walk down the pathway that faces you called **Bell Yard**. At the far end of this path, almost 200 yards away, is a main road—the junction of **The Strand** (to the right) and **Fleet Street** (to the left). The traffic makes this spot too noisy to enjoy for long, but notice, before you go, the compli-

Making a full-bottomed wig

cated monument on the right in the middle of the road. Positioned here in 1880, it has a dragon on top and statues of royalty lower down. The site is called **Temple Bar** and has been for centuries a point of entry into the City of London from Westminster; barriers of various kinds have stood here since the Middle Ages. (As you stand at the bottom of Bell Yard, the City lies to your left, and Westminster to the right.) When a sovereign enters the City from Westminster on a ceremonial occasion, the Lord Mayor of London presents him or her, at Temple Bar, with a sword representing the armed might of the City. The sovereign then gives it back, as if to say, "You use it to look after me." Cross the main road, and from the far side you will see a miniature representation of this scene, sculpted on the side of the monument; Queen Victoria is shown in a carriage, entering the City at the start of her reign in 1837. On horseback and drawing his sword, the Lord Mayor comes to meet her. This ceremony, which occurred again in 1977 at the Jubilee of Elizabeth II, was first recorded in the late sixteenth century. Probably the ceremony goes back to the time when the City was almost an independent little state within England and the sovereign genuinely had to ask permission to enter.

Until the eighteenth century, this busy place was used for displaying the heads of people executed for treason. The heads had to be fastened high up, so that sympathizers could not easily rescue and bury them. But this meant that some people had difficulty making out the features of the dead men's faces. To meet this important need, traders operated here with telescopes. In August 1746 a literary gent named Horace Walpole wrote in a letter, "I have this morning passed under the new heads at Temple Bar, where people make a trade of letting spying-glasses at a halfpenny a look."

A few yards away at no. 3 Fleet Street is an excellent and old-fashioned tobacconist, **Weingott's.** Here since 1859, the shop is furnished in nineteenth-century ma-

Miniature sculpture of Queen Victoria,
Temple Bar, now badly weathered

hogany. Notice also the long wooden counter—a rare survivor. The shop is one of the last in the country to sell
loose tobacco, weighed by hand, in large quantities. There
are brass scales on the counter and rows of earthenware
jars behind. Lawyers from the Temple are among the
main customers. I was told of one well-known judge who
in recent years has bought his snuff here, blended to his
own specifications. Visitors especially favor the large
London-made briar pipes and Havana cigars. The wry
and friendly assistant who told me about the shop (he
asked to be called just "Cyril") has worked in Fleet Street
for over forty years. The square mile or so of the old City,
with its hidden alleyways and courtyards, its long-
established firms and rather polite working people, cre-
ates a loyalty and pride in many of those who know it
well. Cyril told me that he thought it "the finest place to
work in the world."

A few yards farther into the City, on the right, you
will pass the grand seventeenth-century entrance to the
Middle Temple. (To see it properly you may want to
cross the street again for a moment.) It's built in stone
and red brick with pilasters; the Latin inscription means
"This went up at the expense of the Middle Temple
Society, 1684." Forty yards farther along the street,
again on the right, is an even older entrance to the
Temple, which we shall go through in a few minutes.
First, have a look at the partly timbered building above
the entrance, **no. 17**; it's unusual in several ways. It's
one of the very few domestic buildings in London to have
survived from Shakespeare's day—most of the City of
London was destroyed by the Great Fire of 1666,
which stopped just a few yards from here. Permission to
build this house was given in 1610; you will notice that
it overhangs the street slightly—the builder asked to "jettie
out" by twenty-eight inches in addition to the window.
Until the late eighteenth century, houses were usually
not numbered, but many had names and signs instead,
like pubs today. Traces of these old house signs have

Wig & Pen Club, Temple Bar

now almost entirely disappeared; for one thing, in the nineteenth century respectable people didn't want their homes mistaken for pubs! But this building is a rare exception. In the seventeenth century it was named The Prince's Arms, after Prince Henry, the short-lived son of James I. Carved in the woodwork at the front of the house you can see the three feathers, the traditional badge of the Prince of Wales, the heir apparent. In the seventeenth century the building became a tavern for a while, and in 1665, during the Great Plague (which killed about a quarter of London's population), "remedies" for the disease were sold here.

On afternoons during the week, this old house is open to the public. Go up the stairs at the left of the frontage and you will come into a large room overlooking Fleet Street. Wooden paneling and an elaborate plaster ceiling survive from the seventeenth century, and in the middle of the ceiling is another reference to Prince Henry. Although this room has no special connection with Samuel Pepys, it has been interestingly equipped as a memorial to him. On the wall hangs a page from a seventeenth-century satire that attacked Pepys and his clerk, Will Hewer, for the bribes they took at the Navy Office—it mentions gifts of wine, chocolate, anchovies, and oysters.

When you are back in Fleet Street, go through the passage underneath the house, past the newspaper vendors who have a thriving business on weekdays. Once through the passage, you will notice that the noise of Fleet Street falls away, and you are in the Temple.

"**The Temple**" is not the name of a building but means rather the large site which was once the English headquarters of the Templar knights and is now occupied by two adamantly independent Inns of Court. The sites of the **Inner Temple** and **Middle Temple** interlock slightly, as you will see, but the Inner Temple has most of its buildings to the east (left) of the lane

Lawyers' chambers, the Temple

where you now are, while most of the Middle Temple is to the west. Thirty yards down this lane, stop and look at the first staircase on the right. Among the barristers' names you may see that of Mr. John Mortimer, a well-known English liberal and defense lawyer, who is also a successful TV playwright. In the late 1970s and 1980s, Mr. Mortimer created a popular series about an amiable defense barrister, not entirely unlike himself, called "Rumpole of the Bailey." Some of its scenes were shot in this passageway.

Beside the staircase entrances on this block are badges showing the symbol of the Inner Temple: Pegasus, the winged horse. When you are level with the second doorway (no. 2) of the block, turn left and walk 40 yards to the gate that is overgrown with creeper (a climbing, ivy-like plant). On the way you'll see (to the left) **Goldsmith Building,** which belongs to the Middle Temple; above its doorway is a stone version of the Inn's badge: the lamb (symbol of Christ) bearing a flag with the sign of the cross. There will be a lot more lambs and flags (and winged horses) along the way; the authorities of the two Inns are very keen to mark their property. (One lawyer complained recently that the badges were even to be found in lavatories.) The lamb and flag here is protected by mesh from birds, but at the time of this writing the birds are winning. Outside Goldsmith Building are two fine, globular gas lamps. If you look on the board at the entrance, the names of the occupants of the third floor may show you that some rooms in the Inns (and especially those on the top stories) are still residential.

When you reach the overgrown gate, turn left and look at two graves—in very different styles. One, from 1726, is of a lawyer named John Hiccocks. Above his tomb is a large stone effigy of the man, gracefully lounging in his finery: long wig, flared coat, breeches, and bands (strips of cloth at the neck, still worn by barristers). You can't help contrasting this self-advertisement with the real state of the body underneath. In spite of the boastful grave, Hiccocks is almost entirely forgotten.

The other grave, just to the right, is simple and more often visited; it belongs to Oliver Goldsmith, one of the best-known writers of the eighteenth century. An Irishman, Goldsmith had lodgings in the Temple and struggled to pay his debts by producing plays and verse. His comedy *She Stoops to Conquer* is still performed in England; it's about a man who mistakes a house for a pub and treats the worthy occupants of the house as servants. The play is a frequent choice for the dramatic productions of older schoolchildren; there are low-cut dresses and sexual innuendos to keep the kids happy, while Goldsmith's language is old-fashioned enough for the parents to believe the children don't know what's going on.

Goldsmith also wrote a well-known serious poem called "The Deserted Village," the story of a thriving community driven out by a landlord eager to convert his estate to profitable grazing. Goldsmith makes a sentimental but effective contrast between the happy village and the desolate pasture that replaces it. Once there was

> The never-failing brook, the busy mill,
> The decent church that topt the neighbouring hill,
> The hawthorn bush, with seats beneath the shade,
> For talking age and whisp'ring lovers made.

But after the landlord has made his changes, there is solitude and emigration:

> No more thy glassy brook reflects the day,
> But, choked with sedges, works its weedy way . . .
> Sunk are thy bowers in shapeless ruin all,
> And the long grass o'ertops the mouldering wall;
> And, trembling, shrinking from the spoiler's hand,
> Far, far away, thy children leave the land.

Goldsmith was actually buried very close to here, in 1774; the exact site in the churchyard isn't known.

Go back past Goldsmith Building and look at the **Temple Church** on the left. This is the only surviving building from the headquarters of the Templar knights. The oldest section of the church is round, modeled on the church of the Holy Sepulchre in Jerusalem; the Templars also got their name from Jerusalem, where they had a base on the site of the old Temple of Solomon.

The sworn aim of the Templars was to protect the Holy Land in the Christian interest. This meant fighting off Muslims—at which the Templars became famously efficient. Their battle cry, in Latin, had a fine, throbbing "no, no, no" sound: *Non nobis, Domine, non nobis, sed Tuo Nomini da gloriam.* ("Not to us, O Lord, not to us, but to Thy Name give the glory.") Even good Islamic warriors must have had doubts about facing a chanting army of these heavily armed and sex-starved monks.

The Templars were founded in 1118 by a Frenchman, and France remained their chief recruiting ground. Their round church here was consecrated in 1185. The windows are rounded at the top in a Romanesque style brought from Normandy. Turn left to reach the stone porch of the church; underneath is a superb, broad Norman doorway with a receding set of decorated, round arches. The huge hinges on the door form a pleasant design in metal.

The modern entrance to the Temple Church is a few yards farther around to the left. If you go in, in a moment, you will see on the floor medieval effigies of knights who were buried here. Also inside, opposite the modern door, are two vertical slits high in the stonework; these were the meager windows of the tiny penitential cell where disobedient Templars were imprisoned.

But first I suggest going into the passage which runs to the right just beyond the large stone porch. Here, at the first staircase on the left, you may see listed rather few women

Memorial to John Hiccocks,
eighteenth-century lawyer, the Temple

barristers. Even Conservative lawyers have complained recently that women are discriminated against in admissions to chambers. Other less serious complaints were made about the rules for women barristers' dress. Like men, the women have to wear wig and gown in court; there are also to be no bare arms or low necklines. On full-dress occasions, the rules laid down for women Queen's Counsel (nearly always called simply "Q.C.s"—the senior grade of barristers appointed by government committee) are complex. They were reported in W. W. Bolton's *Guide to Conduct and Etiquette at the Bar*:

> Coat, made up of black superfine cloth; the same style as a man's coat except that it should not be skirted but instead be short as in a lady's ordinary suit—black flexible buttons—plain white blouse—lace "frill" and ruffles at wrist—plain black skirt of superfine cloth—black silk stockings—black patent leather ladies' court shoes—cut steel buckles—black silk gown—full-bottomed wig—black silk "wig bag"—white gloves.

As uniforms go, rather flattering and luxurious—though notice the full-length wig!

A few yards farther on, the passage enters **Hare Court**. Here, on the far side, were once the chambers of the most notorious of English lawyers, George Jeffreys, the hanging judge of 1685. Jeffreys made his name as an agent of Charles II and of his brother James II. When the Catholic James became King in 1685 numerous Protestants objected, and some backed a rival claimant to the throne—the Duke of Monmouth, an illegitimate son of the late King Charles. (Charles had so many bastards that they were known collectively as "the fraternity.") Monmouth's army was crushed at Sedgemoor in southwestern England, and Jeffreys was then sent, with colleagues, to judge the captives on behalf of King James. The trials of these rebels were hurried, and confessions were improperly extorted. It seems that about 250 were executed on the judge's orders, and there was much disemboweling and quartering. By bullying a witness Jeffreys managed to get an old lady of about seventy condemned for sheltering a rebel. She was beheaded; it was said afterwards that "she was old and dozy and died without much concern." Luckier rebels were transported on Jeffreys's orders to the West Indies, Carolina, and Virginia. Samuel Pepys wondered how they were to be treated: "whether to be sold entirely, as blacks are to slavery, for their whole lives, or for how long? . . ." Three years later James II fell. His protégé Jeffreys was imprisoned by the new regime, amid great popular rejoicing, and died in the Tower of London. Lawyers today note that Jeffreys was a talented advocate and made some unusually precise legal distinctions. Historians point out that there were other, similar legal murderers—notably in the sixteenth century—who have had much less publicity.

Go back through the passage to the Temple Church. Keep its modern entrance on your left, then walk the length of the courtyard facing you, and through the short tunnel at the end. Once through the tunnel you'll see, about 70 yards ahead, a long line of brick buildings stretching away to the right. This is **King's Bench Walk,** the most easterly part of the Temple, and worth a close look. The previous buildings on this site were destroyed by the Great Fire of London, and some of the present ones were put up shortly afterwards. Go across to **no. 4** and behind its gas lamp you will see the date 1678.

The Great Fire began in early September 1666 on the other side of the City, not far from Tower Hill, and was blown in this direction by a strong east wind. In the previous year there had been another disaster, the plague, and some people thought that this double catastrophe for London was too much of a coincidence—the city was being punished by Heaven. Early in 1666, before the fire, a prophet had foretold religious horrors, after noticing that 666 was the number of the evil beast described in Chapter 13 of the Book of Revelation. When the fire duly came, Puritans seem to have identified the cause of heavenly anger as King Charles, with his relaxed morals, and his Catholic brother, James (then known as the Duke of York). So, to appease the public, James arranged to be seen busily fighting the fire. He came to this part of the Temple and sensibly ordered the use of gunpowder on some of the buildings to create a firebreak. At this point a lawyer appeared and "seeing gunpowder brought, came to the Duke and told him it was against the rules and charter of the Temple that anyone should blow that house with gunpowder." But this was no time for due process of law: "Mr. Germaine, the Duke's Master of the Horse, took a cudgel and beat the young lawyer."

Here in the Temple the Great Fire stopped, partly because of the broad, open space but mainly because the east wind died down. Royalists then used the fact in a religious argument of their own. On the great monument to the fire, erected in the 1670s near London Bridge and still standing, it was written that "the fatal fire stopped, as if ordered by Heaven." God wasn't against King Charles after all.

At **no. 5** King's Bench Walk were the chambers of one of the Inner Temple's best-known lawyers, Lord Chief Justice Mansfield. (We saw one of Mansfield's residences in Lincoln's Inn Fields.) When an eighteenth-century slave owner brought a slave to England and then tried to take him away again by force, it was Mansfield who ruled in 1772 that this was illegal. This judgment was soon afterwards used as a basis for making all slavery in England illegal. In the 1770s Mansfield was associated with a new law which liberalized the treatment of Roman Catholics, and this drew on him the fury of Protestant crowds. Catholicism was thought to mean tyranny—the behavior of Louis XVI of France was encouraging this view at the time—and in 1780 anti-Catholic crowds raged through London for days, led by a young aristocrat, Lord

George Gordon. Mansfield's fine house in Bloomsbury was burned by the rioters; he and his wife narrowly managed to escape out the back.

Go 70 yards down King's Bench Walk, to staircase **no. 9.** In 1888 this contained the chambers of a certain Montague Druitt, a young barrister who seems never to have been given a case. At the end of that year Druitt drowned himself in the Thames. The authorities of the Inner Temple are not likely to give him much publicity; at present he is the leading suspect for identification as Jack the Ripper.

There were probably five Ripper murders, all in the rough East End of London (little more than a mile from here) during the autumn of 1888. The victims were impoverished prostitutes; the Ripper got his name from the indescribable carvings done to their bodies. The killer was never arrested (so far as is publicly known), but a few months after the last murder a policeman in the East End is said to have told a local vigilante that there would be no more such killings and that the murderer had died in the Thames. The private papers of a London police chief of the period suggested that Druitt was the chief suspect. And there is some evidence that there was once a pamphlet written by a Dr. Lionel Druitt, cousin of Montague, and entitled "The East End Murderer—I Knew Him." At the time of the killings it was suspected that the murderer was a man of genteel appearance, able to win the confidence of his later victims because they were on the lookout for a rough "Ripper type." A very poor man might not have been able to find the privacy to wash the bloodstains from himself and his clothes; a man with money could have had a room of his own nearby—perhaps even on this staircase.

Very like Druitt in appearance, with a similar aquiline nose, was the most interesting of his fellow suspects: Prince Albert Victor, grandson of Queen Victoria and elder son of Edward, Prince of Wales (later Edward VII). Had he lived, Albert Victor would have come to the throne on Edward's death in 1910, but he died young, in 1892, after acquiring a strange reputation. Evidence that he was Jack the Ripper was first claimed publicly in 1970, by an eminent, elderly surgeon named Thomas Stowell. Stowell said that his source for the theory was the private papers of Sir William Gull, physician to the Royal Family in the 1880s. Stowell is now dead, and Gull's papers have never been published. A famous government pathologist said fairly recently that he himself disbelieved Stowell's theory but that it had been put to him before Stowell published it by "one of the really great authorities on Jack the Ripper." Buckingham Palace, understandably, has denied the charge that Jack the Ripper might have been the Queen's great-uncle.

Albert Victor, like Druitt, was connected with the Temple; in 1885 he was elected an honorary member of the Middle Temple's governing body. Whether or not either of these men was the Ripper, the Temple was certainly a wild place in the nineteenth century. The residents, many of them not lawyers, were virtually uncontrolled. One prostitute reported that her colleagues were afraid to go there and that a shrewd woman would prefer to jump from a moving cab rather than be taken by a man to the Temple.

Go back up King's Bench Walk for 40 yards, then turn left and cross the wide parking lot to enter the lane directly opposite. The first block on the left is called the **Paper Buildings**; at its entrance (staircase 1) was, until recently, the splendidly Dickensian name of a solicitors' firm, Griffinhoofe and Co. Beyond the Paper Buildings, on the left, are the gardens of the Inner Temple (unfortunately, closed to the public). It was here that Shakespeare imagined the symbolic beginning of the Wars of the Roses, the long fifteenth-century civil wars between the dynastic houses of Lancaster and York. Lancaster was symbolized by the red rose, York by the white. In *Henry VI* Shakespeare describes a quarrel in the Temple garden between the Yorkist character Richard Plantagenet and the Lancastrian Earl of Somerset, in which the emblems were chosen.

> PLANTAGENET: Let him that is a true-born gentleman . . . from off this brier pluck a white rose with me.
>
> SOMERSET: Let him that is no coward nor no flatterer . . . pluck a red rose from off this thorn with me . . .
>
> PLANTAGENET: Hath not thy rose a canker, Somerset?
>
> SOMERSET: Hath not thy rose a thorn, Plantagenet?
>
> PLANTAGENET: . . . by my soul, this pale and angry rose, as cognizance of my blood-drinking hate, will I for ever, and my faction, wear, until it wither with me to my grave, or flourish to the height of my degree.

These gardens were extended in the 1860s, when the making of the Thames Embankment narrowed the river and created new land. At the time there was an official plan to build docks on the river frontage, but the lawyers of the Temple were appalled at this threat to their peace and no doubt applied pressure in high places. A compromise was reached about the new land: no docks, but no large buildings for the lawyers either. So they enlarged their gardens instead.

Pass the elaborate iron gates dated 1730 which lead to the gardens. (Just through the gates you'll see a fine bed of red and white roses in summer.) Continue along the lane until the gardens end; just beyond this point is a stone arch, and on the other side runs **Middle Temple Lane** to the left and right. Turn left into the lane for a moment, and look at the stone buildings which arch across it farther down. These were put up in the 1870s, jointly by the Inner Temple (to the left of the Lane) and the Middle Temple (to the right). The scheme made for increased quarreling between the two bodies. The Inner Temple wanted to build in stone, to match its existing structures; the Middle Temple wanted brick for the same reason. On this point the Inner Temple won. But then came a juicier legal issue: who owned that section of the new building which was directly over the lane? The Inner Temple claimed a share in it, because architecturally it could hardly exist without the adjoining section which is on Inner Temple land. But the Middle Temple argued that because the soil of Middle Temple Lane was *its* property, the building over the lane must also be. Being experienced lawyers, the gentlemen of the two Inns preferred not to settle the issue in court. The Middle Temple took two of the four floors and allowed the Inner Temple to have a lease of the other two for 999 years at a yearly rent of two shillings (a tenth of a pound).

Come back up Middle Temple Lane and turn into the first courtyard that appears on your left, **Fountain Court.** The building on your left as you enter the court is the **hall of the Middle Temple**; it was built in the 1560s and 1570s, during the reign of Elizabeth I. The exterior of the hall was renovated in the eighteenth century, but the interior remains largely as it was in Tudor times. On the roof of the hall is a pretty cupola (also called a lantern); the present one is not the original, but there has been a cupola in this position since the 1570s. Its original use wasn't merely decorative; it had to let out smoke without letting in rain. The fireplace of the hall was in mid-floor; there was no chimney for it—the smoke just wandered upward and drifted out of the cupola.

The Elizabethan naval warrior Sir Francis Drake once staged a grand theatrical entry here. In August 1586, Drake had just returned from a successful expedition (plundering Spanish possessions) and, while the lawyers were dining in the hall, he unexpectedly swept in. He was a member of the Middle Temple, and the records of the Inn (kept in bad Latin) say that he was received with great rejoicing. A few years earlier, Drake and his men had become the first Englishmen to sail round the world; during the voyage they had landed in California and rather optimistically claimed the place for Queen Elizabeth.

In February 1602, almost at the end of the Queen's long reign, there was some real theater here in the hall. A Middle Temple barrister noted in his diary, "February 2nd. At our feast we had a play called *Twelfth Night*, or *What You Will*, much like *The Comedy of Errors* . . ." This is the first recorded performance of Shakespeare's play. Unfortunately, the barrister doesn't mention who the actors were, but it was twenty years before the play was published in print, and it is argued that only Shakespeare's company is likely to have acted from the manuscript version. If so, Shakespeare himself was probably among the actors.

Later in the seventeenth century there were wild disturbances in the hall. The students and young barristers of the Middle Temple used to hold "Grand Christmasses," with much drinking and gambling. (In the eighteenth century, when part of the interior of the hall was renovated, about a hundred ancient dice were discovered, which had been lost in the original floor.) The Grand Christmas of 1629 was especially lively; the authorities of the Inn canceled the celebration for the following year. But the young gentlemen disobeyed, entered the hall and, when the steward refused to bring them food, locked him in the stocks. The authorities retaliated with punishments, at which the students here approached the Benchers in hall to protest. On being turned away, they "hasted down tumultuously, and calling for pots threw them at random toward the Bench table and struck several masters."

In November 1639 the hall was locked to prevent another Grand Christmas. But various members of the Inn "with their swords drawne in a contemptuous and riotous manner assembled themselves and did by violences breake open the dores of the hall, butterie and kitchin and did sett up commons [food] and playe [gambling]." Today's younger barristers and legal students act in striking contrast to their spirited seventeenth-century predecessors. Anxious to be accepted into chambers, or relieved to be there, they are controlled far more by the fear of their elders' disapproval. Unnaturally sedate behavior is the norm, and some young lawyers attempt to look middle-aged prematurely, so as not to put off clients by seeming young and inexperienced.

Outside the hall, under the trees in the courtyard, is a fountain; there has been one here since 1681. Dickens was fond of the place; for him it was a symbol of life amid legal sterility. In *Martin Chuzzlewit* he says:

> Brilliantly the Temple fountain sparkled in the sun, as little Ruth and her companion came towards it. There Tom could see her . . . coming briskly up, with the best little laugh upon her face that ever played in opposition to the fountain. The fountain might have leapt up twenty feet to greet this spring of hopeful maidenhood that in her person stole through the dry and dusty channels of the law. . . .

Psychologists might have something to say about the symbolism here—the springs of maidenhood and leaping (male) fountains; Dickens, as is well known, had an intense imagination!

To the right, in the far corner of Fountain Court just behind the trees, is a gate leading to a pub, **The Devereux.** On summer mornings the path between the pub and the court is often taken over by well-dressed, young-ish legal men with pint glasses in hand. Through the crowd step barristers in twos and threes on their way from the law courts, wigs and gowns removed but white bands still in place at the neck. At the Devereux the strong beer (Director's) is good; this is also a reasonable place for a pub lunch. Better still is **The George,** 50 yards along the passage, to the right.

Perhaps the best place to end this walk is back in Fountain Court. There are seats by the fountain itself, and also a view into the Middle Temple gardens by the end of the hall. Lawyers have occupied the Temple since the fourteenth century. The story of how they came to replace the Templar knights involves one of the greatest crimes of the Middle Ages, and makes a tragic epilogue to the walk.

In 1291 the Templars lost their most respected function—guarding the Holy Land. Acre, the last Christian toehold in Palestine, had fallen to the Muslims. Over the years the Templar order had become very rich, with many thousands of landed estates in western Europe. Because they were wealthy and involved in banking, the knights had made enemies, and after the fall of Acre some of these opponents saw their chance. Chief among them was Philippe IV (Philip the Handsome) of France.

Philippe tried to unite the two main orders of fighting monks, the Templars and the Knights of St. John ("The Hospitallers"), hoping to become the ruler of the large new organization and to gain control of Templar wealth. But the chief of the Templars, a distinguished warrior named Jacques de Molay, opposed this, and Philippe retaliated by organizing a coup. What happened was that on October 12, 1307, de Molay was an honored participant alongside the King at a royal funeral. Early the next morning, Templars were arrested all over France on orders from Philippe issued secretly long before. Shocking confessions then began to emerge; Templars stated that they had denied Christ, spat on the crucifix, taken homosexual vows, and worshiped the devil. Jacques de Molay himself confessed. Philippe now had a case for seizing the vast Templar wealth, which he did.

But were the confessions true? Some Templar knights

who had been captured by Muslims chose to spend years in the jails of Syria and Egypt rather than deny Christ. In confessions about devil worship, it was stated that the devil had taken the form of a black cat, which had afterward disappeared miraculously into a wall. During examination, one Templar revealed the main reason for these strange confessions—by producing the bones of his own foot, roasted off under torture. The knights, including de Molay, had been savagely tortured by the Church authorities to extract "admissions." The Pope at the time, Clement V, was a Frenchman under Philippe's control; he owed his position to the King. He collaborated vigorously in the persecution. Templars were promised their freedom if they confessed, imprisonment and death if they did not.

In England, the young King Edward II at first stated that the charges against the Templars were incredible, and the English Church authorities tended to agree. But Edward was Philippe's son-in-law, and very much under his influence. Philippe and the Pope pressed hard to get the English Templars tortured; claims about Templar wickedness in France would look very strange if in neighboring England the knights were still to be honored as holy men. Some torture was eventually applied in England and the Master of the Temple here, William de la More, died a prisoner in the Tower of London. In England, as in France, the Templar order was dissolved.

There was a strange sequel. In 1314 Jacques de Molay withdrew his confession, saying that his only great shame was to have confessed falsely in the first place. Philippe responded by having him burned on an island in the Seine. But many French people understandably refused to believe the accusations against the Templars: some of the more enthusiastic collected de Molay's ashes and treated them as the relics of a saint. It came to be said that as de Molay died in the flames he cursed King Philippe. Later events certainly suggested the working of a curse: Philippe died within a few months; so did Pope Clement; and in England Edward II, who had eventually joined in the persecutions, was horribly murdered with a red-hot poker (driven into an unmentionable part of his body). Later French monarchs who came to a bad end were regarded as "the accursed kings" (*les rois maudits*), still suffering from the curse of the Templars.

In France the treasures of the Templar knights were never recovered from royal hands. In England the Temple passed during the 1320s into the keeping of the Hospitallers, and they soon let it to the secular lawyers, who have been here ever since. The lawyers of the Temple have, of course, always been largely concerned with the defense of private property. It is ironic that when they first moved to this pleasant and highly valued site it was still very obviously stolen goods—improperly confiscated from the tortured and humiliated monks of war.

Walk · 3

The Old Palace Quarter

ST. JAMES'S

WALK 3: St. James's

Starting Point: Piccadilly Circus tube station
Buses: 3, 6, 9, 12, 13, 14, 15, 19, 22, 38, 53, 88, 159

This busy and fashionable district, best visited on a weekday, has narrow streets, famous shops, and little-known courtyards. It grew up alongside the Tudor palace of St. James's; its grandest thoroughfare, St. James's Street, runs downhill to the palace gates and is lined with eighteenth-century buildings. Just a few yards away, out of view in dark passages, crime and vice used to flourish; one such alley has survived and will be on this route. Gaslit and crowded with humble shops, it keeps its working-class character just a few yards away from the palace.

The palace itself was built by King Henry VIII in the 1530s, during the time of his second, third, and fourth queens. The area then seemed rather remote, away in the fields, several minutes' walk to the west of the palace of Whitehall. For many years St. James's had been used to isolate a colony of leper women. When the King seized the property of Catholic organizations, these women were sent away. Remains of their buildings were found in fairly recent times inside the palace. Several parts of King Henry's structure are still standing; you'll see them toward the end of the walk.

The architecture of the palace is enjoyable but not imposing. Some later monarchs and their subjects became ashamed of St. James's; in the eighteenth century it was criticized by John Fielding (a magistrate, whose brother Henry wrote *Tom Jones*): "The buildings that compose this merely nominal palace (for by all rules of architecture it has no claim to the title) are low, plain, and ignoble, devoid of any exterior beauty. . . . It reflects no honour on the kingdom, and is the jest of foreigners." Many rulers treated St. James's as a reserve palace, Whitehall being the chief one until it was burned in 1698. In the mid-eighteenth century George III was probably rather relieved to move his residence to Buckingham House (later Buckingham Palace), just a few hundred yards away. But some members of the royal family continued to live at St. James's Palace, and ambassadors of foreign states are still called "Ambassadors to the Court of St. James's." Close to the palace you will see an ancient building where ministers of the short-lived Republic of Texas had their legation in the 1840s.

To serve royalty and the numerous courtiers and hangers-on, shops of unusual quality were opened in the area. Some of them are still in business after two centuries or more. Most of the shops in St. James's charge high prices, as they probably always have. But unlike posh shops in other parts of Britain, their atmosphere isn't overpoweringly grand. For one thing, property has long been so expensive here that even stylish businesses have traditionally been squeezed into narrow and homely buildings.

Some of the finest old houses lie in quiet passages off St. James's Street. On the way to them we shall look at this street itself; although loud and busy nowadays, it contains some of the world's oldest and most exclusive gentlemen's clubs. These places have for centuries provided lodging, drink, and food for the aristocracy and gentry. Only in the last few years have women been allowed in, whether as members or guests. In the eighteenth century politicians and men of fashion gambled here, sometimes in public view, for almost unimaginably large fortunes. Although housed in impressive buildings, these clubs don't display their names outside; the idea perhaps is that *gentlemen* know where the clubs are, and the others . . . well, why tell them?

From Piccadilly tube station, walk 150 yards down the left side of Piccadilly itself, until you reach the railings of the churchyard of **St. James's.** Go in through the gateway to look at the church itself. It was designed by Christopher Wren, the most fashionable architect of the late seventeenth century, and was built between 1676 and 1684. The exterior is plain—too plain for many people's tastes; Wren was under pressure to economize and reserved the elaboration for the interior. The outdoor pulpit next to the church wall was put up in 1902, in the last days of horse-drawn traffic and just before the noise of motors in Piccadilly made it virtually unusable. Before entering, go around to the right of the church tower. On the keystone of the arch you will see a coat of arms showing stars and a crescent moon. This was the badge of Henry Jermyn, Earl of St. Albans, the chief contributor of funds for building the church. Helped by his influence at court, he also took the lead in laying out many of the fine streets of St. James's. He was a friend of Henrietta Maria, widow of the executed King Charles I and mother of the reigning Charles II. It was rumored at court that Charles II wanted Jermyn to join him in a ménage à trois with the royal mistress Barbara Villiers. (More on this rapacious lady later, when we reach the site of her mansion near the palace.) Go up the steps into the garden of the church. From here, under the plane trees, you get an unusual view of the narrow and chic Jermyn Street, which runs below. When you are in the street (in a few minutes)

you'll probably give most of your attention to the shop fronts. But from here you notice more easily the tall and elegant façades, from the eighteenth and nineteenth centuries, which rise above the shops.

In the late eighteenth century the area near the church became very dangerous at night. In 1774 an extra ten watchmen were hired by the parish and provided with cutlasses, carbines and wooden noisemakers to raise the alarm. In 1793 still more watchmen were employed, to deal with "the alarming increase of a most daring and desperate set of thieves, who are harbored in and nightly infest this parish." In the dark streets even time-consuming crimes went on in public; in the 1790s a parish committee here was troubled by numerous thefts of iron railings.

Go back to the church tower, and enter by the door facing Piccadilly. Just inside, on the left, is a modern plaque in honor of the poet and artist William Blake, who was baptized here in 1757. Blake became highly fashionable in Britain in the late 1960s, when pale and long-haired young men, who looked like radicals but were not, found satisfaction in his white, elongated figures.

Inside the church, with its side galleries and rounded baroque arches, Wren's general design is still clear. Many details were restored after the bombing in 1940. Four thousand books of gold leaf were used to gild the new ceiling. Wren was proud of the original interior; writing about St James's, he explained why Protestant churches such as this needed to be small: to allow the worshippers to see and hear all the proceedings, and thus to have informed consciences. (An informed conscience, rather than a priest, was thought by Protestants to be the proper link with God.) "The Romanists may build larger churches; it is enough if they hear the murmur of the mass and see the elevation of the host, but ours are to be fitted for auditories."

In spite of Wren's pious purpose, this church was soon being used for unholy social display. One traveler complained in 1722 that renting a seat during a service cost almost the same as a seat at the theater. Nevertheless, the expense was justified "on a holiday or Sunday, when the fine assembly of beauties and quality come there." Earlier, in 1703, the diarist John Evelyn referred to St. James's as one of the "theatrical churches." Thieves were attracted; in 1693 the authorities here paid ten shillings, a large sum, to a man named Simmonds "for his care in looking after and taking pickpockets in the church."

On entering the body of the church, turn left toward the white marble font, where Blake was christened. Around the stem are carved Adam, Eve and the serpent. This is the work of Grinling Gibbons, the master carver of Wren's day. Gibbons also did the very ornate carving in limewood around the altar.

Go along the wall of the church on the side by the font. Beneath the second window is a memorial to one of the last British colonial administrators in America, Guy Johnston, "of Guy Park in the Province of New York," who, with typical eighteenth-century nepotism, "succeeded his father-in-law as superintendent of Indian affairs in North America" in 1774. He died fourteen years later—in London.

Just past the fourth window in the same wall is a plaque commemorating a society physician of the early nineteenth century, the baronet Sir Richard Croft. As often happens with pious memorials, the really interesting details aren't recorded. Slim and elegant, Croft was involved, to his cost, in a far-reaching tragedy within the Royal Family. In 1817 Princess Charlotte, only child of George, the Prince Regent, and his estranged wife, Caroline, was due to give birth. Croft was the most noted *accoucheur* of the day and was appointed to look after her. He put the poor woman on an insubstantial diet and had her bled liberally, to counter what he called her "morbid excess of animal spirits." After being in labor

Outdoor pulpit, St. James's Church

for fifty hours, Charlotte produced a stillborn child. She herself seemed to make a good recovery at first, but after a few hours she relapsed and died for reasons that have never been fully understood. Croft's reputation was ruined. The Prince Regent kindly published a tribute to him, but there was much hostile criticism in the newspapers. A few months later, in February 1818, when attending the confinement of a woman with symptoms similar to Charlotte's, Croft took a pistol from the wall of the patient's house and shot himself. The body of a suicide was not allowed burial in holy ground, and you will notice that the memorial here was put up many years after Croft's death, when the manner of it had ceased to be notorious. In Croft's day, unpopular suicides were still being buried at crossroads, with a stake driven through the heart.

For the Royal Family, the effects of Charlotte's death could hardly have been greater. Had she lived and had descendants, she—and they—would almost certainly have inherited the throne rather than Charlotte's cousin Victoria and her descendants, who have held the throne from 1837 to the present day.

Going back into the vestibule of the church, you will notice a bell rope, with decorative colored grip, which passes through the ceiling and hangs here. Turn left and you'll come out into Jermyn Street. Across the street, and a few yards to the left, is the start of **Duke of York Street**; go down this for a moment. The first entry on the left is **Apple Tree Yard,** now a dull reality with a pretty name. On the corner of Apple Tree Yard is **Wheeler's,** one of a small chain of respected oyster restaurants. They are decorated in a uniform of green paint, with latticework on the windows.

On the opposite side of Duke of York Street, close to Ormond Yard, is perhaps the finest pub in the area, **The Red Lion.** Look at it first from Wheeler's corner. The present building is mainly from the early nineteenth century. It is four-storied, with a flat front and rounded garret

Seventeenth-century font, St. James's Church

windows on the top floor. The doors gleam with brass, and even from outside you get a hint of the precious etched glass within. The first story was converted in late Victorian times to form a "gin palace," glittering with glass and mirrors. Historic buildings such as this are systematically described in the long and authoritative series of volumes called *Survey of London*. Its authors are usually extremely sober in their language, but when they reach The Red Lion excitement takes over: "The small interior has a ceiling of cigar-brown lincrusta [embossed oilcloth], the walls and partitions being formed in light arcaded frames of polished mahogany, enclosing glass panels enriched in every possible way[!] with frosted, brilliant-cut and partly mirrored arabesque designs." If you like the old-fashioned English beer, flat and strong, the brew to ask for here is Burton.

At the corner with **Jermyn Street** is a men's clothing shop with pleasantly colored tiles running in bands between its windows. Gents' clothes and shoes are among the expensive specialties of Jermyn Street. Turn left at the corner, and notice **no. 93** Jermyn Street (in a building partly of the late seventeenth century), the firm of **Paxton and Whitfield**. Notice the brass plates below the window, stretching almost the length of the façade, on which the engraved name of the business has faded with polishing over the years. The firm describes itself, with old-fashioned vagueness, as "provision merchants" but in fact has an international reputation for one thing—cheese. In the window are whole cheeses, especially popular being Blue Stilton, a strong cheese much sought after in the restaurants of Paris, and made only in northeast Leicestershire, a district of the English Midlands. I found the staff very friendly, and customers are encouraged to taste before buying. The sawdust on the floor doesn't mean that the place is rough-and-ready; it's a reminder that the business claims to give excellent old-fashioned service.

Cheeses and hams, Jermyn Street

Four doors along, at **no. 89,** is **Floris** the perfumers, with a discreet window display and a large, bright, and coarsely executed royal coat of arms above it, to boast of an exalted patron. Floris has traded here since 1810. Look through the door at the lovely old display cases. The building next door, **no. 88,** was largely rebuilt about the year 1800, but parts of it remain from the late seventeenth century when it was the home (from 1696 to 1700) of Isaac Newton, one of the greatest of all physicists. It was Newton, for example, who formulated the laws which apply when a vehicle stops abruptly and the driver keeps going. Today it is fashionable among historians to study Newton's less scientific activities. He was a convinced Unitarian and had to be secretive about this to avoid persecution. He also spent much time carefully examining the accuracy of Old Testament prophecies. In 1700 Newton moved one door down to no. 87, now entirely rebuilt; there is a plaque in his honor.

Across the road at **no. 40** is the slightly lurid entrance to an exclusive and much-publicized disco, **Tramp.** (St. James's is a posh enough district for the name Tramp to be chic and acceptable. In Covent Garden or Soho people might think twice about opening a club with a name like that: they just might get some of the genuine article appearing at the door.)

On the right of the street is the rear section of **Fortnum and Mason's,** one of Britain's grandest general stores. Tea at Fortnum's (on the first and fourth stories) is a favorite social occasion. The cakes here are especially delicious.

If you're near Fortnum's just before the clocks are due to strike the hours, you may like to turn right here and go for a moment to the front of the building, in Piccadilly. On the third story of the façade is a large ornamental clock. On the hour it chimes delicately; double-leaved miniature doors open on each side, and two mechanical

Shopping arcade, Jermyn Street

figures appear, dressed in the livery of eighteenth-century servants, holding a tray and lighted candles. The tune played by the bells is the song of Eton school. Very touristy, but pretty. Back in Jermyn Street, a few yards farther down on the right, is another reference to Eton. The clothing shop **New and Lingwood,** at the entrance to Piccadilly Arcade, advertises that it "incorporates W. V. Brown of Eton."

Eton is a resonant name in English ears; a small town to the west of London, close to the royal residence of Windsor Castle, Eton contains by far the best-known and most aristocratic of private schools. To have attended Eton often causes one to have one's name mentioned in the gossip columns. Wealthy Englishmen have traditionally defended the privileges of Eton; in the nineteenth century the Duke of Cumberland, one of Queen Victoria's uncles, tried to prevent the building of the Great Western Railway on the grounds that the noise from it would disturb the Eton boys.

A little farther along, Jermyn Street is joined by **Bury Street** (pronounced "berry"). Bury Street has existed since the late seventeenth century, but its present buildings are relatively new. The freehold of the street is owned by the crown, and the *Survey of London* complains discreetly but persistently about the crown's policy here of demolishing old buildings. In February 1755 there was a dramatic fire in the street, described in a gossipy letter by Horace Walpole:

> I am at present confined with a cold, which I caught by going to a fire in the middle of the night, and in the middle of the snow, two days ago. About 5 in the morning Harry waked me with a candle in his hand, and cried, "Pray, your honour, don't be frightened!" "No, Harry, I am not: but what is it that I am not to be frightened at?" "There is a great fire here in St. James's St." I rose, and indeed thought all St. James's St. was

on fire, but it proved in Bury Street. However, you know I can't resist going to a fire: for it is certainly the only horrid sight that is fine. I slipped on my slippers, and an embroidered suit that hung on the chair, and ran to Bury St., and stepped into a pipe that was broken up for water. It would have made a picture—the horror of the flames, the snow, the day breaking with difficulty through so foul a night, and my figure—mud and gold. There were two houses burnt, and a poor maid; another jumped out of a window and is much hurt, and two young beauties were conveyed out the same way in their shifts.

Seeing young beauties in their nightclothes was one of the rewards of fire gazing, or fire fighting. In the late nineteenth century fire fighting became highly fashionable. The head of the London fire brigade was a glamorous public figure, and the Prince of Wales (later King Edward VII) served as an amateur fireman. One famous advertisement of the time showed a brawny fire fighter descending a rope with a thinly clad beauty fainting over his arm.

At the far left corner of Jermyn Street and Bury Street is a well-known shop for men's shirts, **Turnbull and Asser.** Over the doorways are prettily painted cherubs. From across the street, look upwards at some imaginative architecture from the early twentieth century. The area above the shop has been designed to resemble an Italian Renaissance tower of seven stories; near the top a miniature colonnade of windows forms an imitation loggia.

A few yards farther, Jermyn Street ends in **St. James's Street.** Although St. James's Street is noisy and traffic-ridden, some of its buildings are worth a look before you go on to quieter places. Turn to the right for a moment. The eighteenth-century building at **no. 37** (two doors up from Jermyn Street) is **White's,** one of the most famous English clubs for wealthy gentlemen. The club has been on this site since 1755 and began as a chocolate house in the late seventeenth century, when cocoa was expensive and fashionable. (Supplies of cocoa were said to have been among the bribes offered to Samuel Pepys at the seventeenth-century Navy Office.) Notice the fine lamps at the club door, and the iron boot scrapers.

In the late eighteenth century White's was a club for Tories, the country party of conservatives who supported King George III. The rival, reformist Whigs had their club across the road at **Brooks's.** (Brooks's is still there, 80 yards down the hill—the building of yellow-gray stone with flat pillars built into its frontage. We shall reach it in a moment.) In February 1784 the young Tory Prime Minister, William Pitt, was on his way back from a dinner given in his honor by the Grocers' Company, when he was attacked outside Brooks's by a gang, probably hired by the Whigs. After taking a beating, he narrowly escaped into White's. A Whig poet wrote gleefully:

> *See the sad sequel of the Grocers' treat;*
> *Behold him darting up St. James's Street!*
> *Pelted and scared by Brooks's hellish sprites,*
> *And vainly fluttering round the door of White's.*

At this period there was extravagant gambling at White's, as at neighboring clubs. (The fashionable term for heavy gambling was "deep play.") A poet made a character say:

> *Had I whole counties, I to White's would go,*
> *And set land, woods and rivers at a throw.*

This wasn't a great exaggeration; large landed estates were often lost in an evening's gambling in St. James's Street. Among the favorite games were faro (pronounced "pharoah") and basset. In both, the players bet on the order in which certain cards would be taken from the top of the deck. In the 1730s the satirical artist William Hogarth portrayed (in a series called "Rake's Progress") a young gambler being arrested for debt in this part of St. James's Street: the gambler steps, shocked, out of his sedan chair to meet the bailiff while a lamplighter, filling an oil lamp nearby, looks on in fascination and spills his oil into the street. As a comment on the feverish gambling of the area, Hogarth also showed small children betting at cards on the sidewalk. In the background to the scene is the Tudor gate house of St. James's Palace. Look down the street, and you will see it's still there.

Go back to the corner with Jermyn Street and continue for 60 yards down St. James's Street. At **no. 28** (on the left) is perhaps the finest building in the district. It is flanked by two tall wings, like towers, and in the center is a high Venetian window, rising between miniature Ionic columns and surmounted by a great fan. This is, and has been since 1783, **Boodle's Club.** The building was originally constructed in the previous decade for another club, the Savoir Vivre, which had among its members the infamous General Richard Smith. Smith, a cheesemonger's son from Jermyn Street, had earlier been sent to India, like a lot of other wild young men whose families weren't altogether appalled by the thought that they might never come back. But Smith did come back, with a military title and a fortune. He then tried to set himself up as a Member of Parliament, using bribery so blatantly that even in the corrupt eighteenth century he managed to get sent to prison for it. With his Indian wealth, Smith also became "the deepest of all deep gamesters in London." Horace Walpole describes how Smith and "a set of sharpers" established the Savoir Vivre in this building, forming "a plan for a new club, which, by the excess of play, should draw all the young extravagants thither. They built a magnificent house in St. James's Street, furnished it gorgeously. . . ." Smith and his colleagues were anxious that rich young gamblers should not be restricted in their betting by shortage of ready cash. So, "the titular master of the house the first night

Boodle's, eighteenth-century gambling club, St. James's Street

acquainted the richest and most wasteful of the members that they might be furnished in the house with loans of ready money, even as far as £40,000." (An ordinary person at that time could live on £50 a year.)

Smith's Savoir Vivre Club was not a success, and after

seven years Boodle's took over the premises. This club took its name from Edward Boodle, a genial old scoundrel who had managed it in earlier days (he died in 1772). Boodle had squandered his own large inheritance and enjoyed teaching young men to drink heavily. He made it difficult to escape from his private parties: "when he perceived his young guests begin to flag or become drowsy, he would get up, lock the door of the room and, putting the key in his pocket, strike up the song, ' 'Tis not yet day.' "

Look up at the room on the second story, immediately to the left of the grand Venetian window and above the doorway. This is the "Undress Dining-Room"—for dining in informal clothes. Behind the Venetian window itself is the saloon, one and a half stories high.

In the late 1970s, the membership of Boodle's included Mr. John Profumo, once a luckless politician. When Secretary of State for War in 1963, he was disgraced for having an affair with Christine Keeler, an attractive and very young woman who was also socializing at the time with a Russian agent named Ivanov. The fall of Profumo, all the more spectacular after his public denial of the affair, was a landmark in British social history. Heavy informal censorship and respect for politicians had lingered since the Second World War. In 1963 they were largely swept aside. The infant satire industry became established, launching David Frost and, more important, the magazine *Private Eye*—still a most effective chronicle of British misdeeds in high places. Even the government report into the Profumo affair was saucily written, with paragraph headings that read like a novel: " 'He's a liar,' " " 'The swimming pool,' " "The 'darling' letter" and "Paul Mann takes a holiday." Mr. Profumo was unfortunate to make his mistake at a time when Britain was ripe for a scandal. He has now been partly forgiven as a result of charitable work and recently received a high civil honor.

Cross St. James's Street here, to **Brooks's Club** opposite. This was built in 1778 for the Whig politicians who, led by Charles James Fox, sympathized with the American Revolution. Outside the club are two lead water butts, now used to grow shrubs. Under the foliage you'll see molded in the lead a significant date for the Whigs—1776. Also shown is a scene of St. George killing the dragon, symbolizing the defeat of tyranny by the patron saint of England. The American revolutionaries were regarded as fellow Englishmen by radicals in England, who looked forward to the day when they too could throw off the rule of King George III. A group of politicians in England advertised a collection of money on behalf of "the widows, orphans and aged parents of our beloved American fellow-subjects, who, faithful to the character of Englishmen, preferring death to slavery, were for that reason only inhumanly murdered by the king's troops at or near Lexington and Concord."

The first-story windows at Brooks's are low enough for passersby to stare in, and this in the early 1780s caused much scandal. For, just behind the windows, famous members of the club were gambling for enormous stakes at faro. One critic wrote, "The whole town as it passes views the dealer and the punters, by means of the candles, and the windows being levelled with the ground." (The word *punter* is still common British slang, meaning "gambler" or "customer.") In 1781 Fox himself, with a partner, won over £4,000 here at faro in one night. Sadly for him, his numerous creditors took this as a sign that he was now worth threatening. Bailiffs converged on his nearby house, carted off his property and held it for ransom.

Go 40 yards farther down St. James's Street (in the direction of the palace gate house), then turn right and go through the covered passage into **Blue Ball Yard,** one of the most pleasant and unexpected corners of this district. The yard probably got its name from the sign of a neighboring pub or house in the eighteenth century. It is gaslit and paved with flagstones which slope towards the center, for drainage. The two-story buildings on the left side were almost certainly built in 1741–42 as wine vaults and stables for an aristocrat named Francis Godolphin.

Lead water tank; eighteenth-century English radicals celebrate the American Revolution, St. James's Street

The first story, where horses and coaches were once kept, is now used as a garage; some of the wooden doors are old and irregular, but they are massively fortified. Above the former stables is a single residential story with a sharply angled roof, more reminiscent of a country cottage than an urban yard. Shrubs, tomatoes, and flowers grow in pots along the gallery outside the second story.

Go back into St. James's Street, turn right, and after

30 yards you will come to **St. James's Place**. Go in, and after a few yards turn left into the courtyard by the entrance to **Dukes Hotel**. The courtyard, largely hidden from the road outside, has a wall delightfully covered by climbing plants. Amid the greenery are two gas lamps.

Return to St. James's Place. This street was laid out in the 1680s and 1690s, and some of its original buildings survive. **No. 11**, on the far side, was the scene of a violent quarrel in 1698, when the owner was erecting outbuildings in his garden. Neighbors, belonging to the lordly Godolphin family, objected that their privacy was being invaded and threatened the workmen "with a pistol ready cocked." The present building at no. 11 was put up in the early 1780s, though it has been altered since. In 1820 it became the home of a successful cartoonist, whose influence is still evident. His name was Robert Cruikshank, and he, with his brother George, did the original "Tom and Jerry" cartoons. These cartoons appeared in 1820–21, in a series called "Life in London." The heroes of the drawings were not cat and mouse; they were two wild young men-about-town. "Jerry" was thought at the time to be modeled on Robert Cruikshank himself, and "Tom" on George. Tom and Jerry were shown in fashionable and outrageous scenes—eyeing the stylish courtesans of Covent Garden, meeting "Flashy Nance," the whore who could outdrink a sailor, and cutting a figure in a gin shop, where "blue ruin," a mixture of gin and fruit cordial, was a favorite drink of the day. Especially popular was a cartoon that showed Tom and Jerry, attended by two hopeful and elaborately dressed young prostitutes, playing a practical joke on a "charley." (Charleys were the predecessors of bobbies—watchmen, often elderly, who stood in sentry boxes at night and tried to keep order in the streets.) Jerry and the two women look on while a grinning Tom pushes over a watchman's box from behind. The charley falls forward, followed by the sentry box, which pins him helplessly to the ground.

The cartoons were a huge success. "Tom and Jerry" hats appeared in London. Pirate editions of the drawings were sold across the Atlantic, making the phrase "Tom

and Jerry" widely known in America. Tom and Jerry behavior was also copied, with serious results for charleys.
There was an outbreak of charley-baiting throughout
London; one observer noted that even in a quiet suburb
"the watchman's box was on several occasions toppled
over on its slumbering inmate, by parties of young bloods
fresh from flowing bowls of punch. . . ." Another critic
claimed that Tom and Jerry "had a great deal to answer
for in the way of leading soft-headed young men astray."

George Cruikshank had already become famous as a political cartoonist; he was especially fond of showing the Prince
Regent (later George IV) with careful attention to the Prince's
vast waist and rear. The more scandalous of these cartoons
were so wounding that a secret royal payment of £100 was
made to the artist in 1820, in return for a promise "not to
caricature His Majesty in any immoral situation." George
Cruikshank was probably more radical than his brother Robert, but he enjoyed the expensive and dissipated way of life
shown in the "Tom and Jerry" cartoons. According to his
publisher, he was addicted to "late hours, blue ruin and dollies." Later in the nineteenth century, when the shocking
Georgian court had been replaced with Queen Victoria's propriety, George Cruikshank publicly renounced drink and became a temperance campaigner. Many other Victorians were
ashamed to look back on their own pre-Victorian pasts, and
the novelist Thackeray had fun imagining an innocent Victorian child questioning its now-respectable grandparents
about their doings in the heyday of Tom and Jerry:

> Grandmamma, did you wear such a dress as that
> when you danced? . . . There was very little of it,
> grandmamma! Did grandpapa kill many watch
> men when he was a young man, and frequent
> thieves, gin-shops, cock-fights and the ring before
> you married him? He is very much changed. He
> seems a gentlemanly old boy now.

Nos. 13 and **14**, a little farther along St. James's Place,
are the best preserved of the small buildings in the street.

No. 14 is a late-seventeenth-century structure, though its front has been given a later coat of stucco (a plaster made of lime, portland cement, and sand). In front of the flat first story, two thin iron pillars support the bay front of the second and third, producing a ramshackle elegance.

Opposite these houses the street opens into a wide space where horses and carriages could comfortably turn. On the far side is **no. 28,** a magnificent flat-fronted town house, dating mainly from the late eighteenth century. There is an intricately patterned fanlight above the door, and outside is a superb array of antique lighting equipment. On each side of the entrance is a conical torch extinguisher in iron. Above are two metal loops which once held the glass globes of oil lamps. And, standing out from the wall, is a functioning light of the sort which, in the early nineteenth century, made both torches and oil lamps obsolete—gas.

The blue plaque at no. 28 mentions that this was once the home of a politician named William Huskisson. In an age when several of his eminent colleagues were notorious for drinking and dueling, Huskisson was a more sober character. The best-remembered episode of his life is his departure from it. In 1830, he attended a ceremony to open the Liverpool-to-Manchester railway. But, while anxiously scrambling out of the way of an approaching locomotive called "The Rocket," he fell out of a carriage and his leg was run over. He died in great pain a few hours later.

Next door to Huskisson's narrow and elegant brick house is a building in a very different style, **no. 27, Spencer House.** Far wider, it is built of yellowish stone with flat pilasters and classical columns. The architect, John Vardy, was originally hired to build a great house here by one Henry Bromley, the first Baron Montfort. But the plan fell through: Bromley got into financial trouble, called his lawyer, carefully read over his will and then shot himself before the lawyer had time to leave. Later, in the 1760s, Vardy found another client, John Spencer (later

Earl Spencer). This young man had fallen in love before being of an age to marry; his wedding took place on the day after he came of age, yet in one of the rooms of this house he commissioned a painting showing a secret marriage. Look through the window just beyond the door at the glittering gilded ceiling.

Behind (to the south of) Spencer House was once Cleveland House, a mansion owned by Barbara Villiers, Duchess of Cleveland. She was one of the greediest and most notorious of Charles II's mistresses and was also extremely beautiful. During the great plague of 1665, Samuel Pepys, while terrified of dying, had a dream about holding Barbara in his arms. He concluded that if dying meant entering a dreamlike existence of that kind, death wouldn't be such a bad thing after all.

Go across the road to where St. James's Place bends to the right and runs uphill for about 100 yards. At the top of the little hill, on the left, is a modern building, **no. 21.** This site was once the northwest corner of Barbara Villiers's garden, and in 1956, when the present building was being erected, interesting traces of her luxurious life-style were found here. A pit—nearly thirteen feet deep and more than thirteen feet in diameter at the top—was discovered; its sides sloped inwards as they descended and were lined with bricks. This was an icehouse, built in 1668 or soon afterwards, and at the time known more prettily as a "snow well." In winter, ice and snow were packed into it; deep below ground, they remained frozen for much of the summer, enabling wine and food to be lowered in and chilled. This idea was brought from Italy and France, and probably was first used in England in the early 1660s, soon after the restoration of Charles II. The first royal snow well, built not far from here, was eagerly saluted by a court poet, Edmund Waller:

Yonder the harvest of cold months laid up,
Gives a fresh coolness to the royal cup;

> *There ice like crystal, firm and never lost,*
> *Tempers hot July with December's frost.*
> *Winter's dark prison; whence he cannot fly,*
> *Though the warm Spring, his enemy, grows nigh.*
> *Strange! that extremes should thus preserve the snow,*
> *High on the Alps, and in deep caves below.*

Five snow wells were built for the King on the sites of nos. 22–25 St. James's Place, but they seem not to have worked satisfactorily; before 1700 they were allowed to fall into disrepair.

Next door, at the end of St. James's Place and looking down the hill, is **no. 20**—still gaslit at the front. Go past it to the small blind alley that runs from the right of the street. Here, 3 yards past the door of **no. 19**, look at the tiny window about 6 feet from the ground. It measures approximately 11 × 10 inches but across it is set a stout iron bar—to keep out any little Artful Dodgers. No. 19 also has some fragile-looking but attractive bow windows.

Come back down St. James's Place, passing (on the right) the small alley which dives under no. 21 and comes up again at the edge of Green Park. Follow the road around to the left, until you emerge again into St. James's Street. Cross the street and go right; the block just beyond King Street contains three of London's best-known and oldest specialty shops: Lobb's the shoemakers, Lock's the men's hatters, and the wine merchants Berry Bros. and Rudd. All three serve the royal court, and I confess that I expected their staff to be fearfully grand—many posh English shops depend on intimidation to impress customers. Instead I found quiet manners and an interest in getting the product right according to the producer's own high standards as well as those of the customer.

By the door of **Lobb's**, at **no. 9** St. James's Street, in a little window to the right, is an excerpt from a Victorian publication, recording that Lobb's won the only gold medal for boot making at the Paris Exhibition of 1867:

"The jurors declared they never saw such beautiful work-manship and style." The business has existed since 1850. The founder, John Lobb, was a Cornishman who brought back the capital to open his London store after a successful stay in Australia, where he had designed a "prospector's boot" for the gold diggers—of ordinary appearance but with a hollow heel for nuggets and gold dust. Lobb's descendants still run the firm.

A few yards farther, at **no. 6**, is **Lock's,** which claims to be the oldest surviving hatter's business in the world. It has been in St. James's Street since the late seventeenth century, and in its present building since 1765. The plain and dignified shop front has delicate and slightly irregular bars dividing the windows; below these a grille of hefty iron reaches down to the sidewalk, allowing light to the basement while keeping out thieves. Notice, too, the ancient (and valued) dents in the door. Always on show in the left-hand window are some of Lock's tall hats from the early nineteenth century—similar, by the way, to those shown in the "Tom and Jerry" cartoons. The two light-colored hats are called "beavers," the dark ones "silk." In the right-hand window is a three-cornered ("tricorn") hat, of a type well known in Britain and America from eighteenth-century paintings. These antiques aren't for sale. Lock's still makes some military caps (you will see specimens from bygone ages in the window); famous British warriors who have been customers here include the commanders in the Napoleonic Wars, Admiral Lord Nelson and the Duke of Wellington.

Ten yards farther, at **no. 3** St. James's Street, is the wine shop of **Berry Bros. and Rudd.** The alleyway beside it leads to a charming eighteenth-century courtyard, as we shall see in a moment. First, though, look at the front of the shop. On weekends and in the evenings only the arched tops of the first-story windows are visible, the rest being hidden by thick wooden shutters which date, like the building itself, from the eighteenth century. Underneath their glossy black paint the shutters have numerous

Four kinds of old lighting equipment—gaslight, oil light, fanlight, and torch extinguisher, St. James's Place

scars, some of them dating from 1940, when a stick of bombs hit the area. Among those killed was a sentry outside St. James's Palace, 100 yards away.

On a weekday, look through the windows at the austerely elegant interior. The floor is of bare boards, and there are no modern wine bottles on display. But to the right are black, antique bottles, and also a display of miniature bottles, which are scarcely an inch high. These miniatures were made in the 1920s when Queen Mary, wife of King George V and a compulsive collector, employed one of the firm's directors to equip a dollhouse with its own cellar of wine. Great ingenuity was used in producing the tiny bottles and their labels, and in filling them with the corresponding wines by pipette—the necks of the bottles being too narrow otherwise to allow in even small drops of wine.

From the ceiling of the shop hang two weighing beams, both from the eighteenth century. The smaller one is still in use for a custom which has existed here since the 1760s: weighing clients. Until the late nineteenth century few scales were available elsewhere for personal measurement, and many grand people came here for the purpose. Some insisted on being weighed naked, for greater accuracy. The records, handwritten and carefully preserved in the shop in large ledgers, note very properly that in such cases the shop was closed at the time. Clothing and diet were also noted, sometimes in obsessive detail. (Weight watching was thought an important guide to health; also, in an age of aristocratic indulgence, there was a widespread and often reasonable dread of getting fat.) One nineteenth-century grandee, the 4th Baron Rivers, had his weight recorded here nearly five hundred times. For example: "1864, July 27th, 12 stone 4 lbs. at 1:30; 12 stone 5 lbs. at 2 p.m. after two chops and a pint of sherry."

Among the most interesting records in the ledgers are those recalling the weight of George III's sons, the gigantic Hanoverian princes sometimes called "Queen Victoria's wicked uncles." The Duke of Wellington once referred to these men as "the damnedest millstones that were ever hanged round the neck of any government." Their measurements help to explain his remark. The second eldest of the royal brothers, the Duke of York, weighed 204 1/2 pounds (in shoes) in 1800. He distinguished himself as a reformer at the head of the British army until 1809, when it was discovered that his mistress, Mary Anne Clarke, had appointed officers in return for bribes. The Duke had to resign his military post in a cloud of scandal. His brother William (later King William IV) weighed 189 pounds (in boots) in 1800. He was a man of lively appetites, fathering at least ten children, none of them legitimate. Look at the top of the gate house of the palace, and you'll see a large clock restored during his reign, bearing the letters WR—William Rex (King)— and the date, 1832. Another brother, the imposing and tyrannical Duke of Cumberland, weighed 189 pounds (in boots) in 1799. More about him later; two of his personal enemies were to die in appalling circumstances, and many in England were relieved when he was sent away to become King of Hanover. A more popular brother, the Duke of Cambridge, weighed 226 1/2 pounds in 1822. Queen Victoria's father, the Duke of Kent, weighed 232 1/2 pounds.

The oldest and most important of the brothers is the only one not to have his weight recorded here: George, Prince of Wales, Prince Regent and later King George IV. His vast proportions and prospective health were a matter of national importance (and of international satire), and were perhaps too sensitive to be entrusted even to the discreetly guarded registers of no. 3. But the Prince was a customer. So too was his satirical opponent, George Cruikshank, and one of Cruikshank's most famous cartoons shows a massive, blubbery sea creature with the unmistakable royal face—the Prince of Whales, of course.

Go down the alleyway to the left of Berry's. Its walls are paneled for the first six feet from the ground;

above that, on the right, you can see how the wall is built with timber filled in with brick. At the entrance to the alley on the right is a modern plaque that was made in San Antonio. It records that the building contained the Texan legation between 1842 and 1845, at the time when Texas was an independent republic. The wine business was suffering in the general depression of the 1840s ("the hungry '40s"), and the American tenants were welcome.

At the end of the alley is **Pickering Place**, a tiny courtyard named after William Pickering who, in the 1730s, constructed most of the buildings that survive, including the one occupied by Berry's. Look at the intricate eighteenth-century doorcases, in wood, at **nos. 3** and **4**. There is no rear entry to these buildings, and if you look through the windows you will see that their rooms are very small. Pickering was squeezing the maximum number of buildings into his little plot. High above the entries to nos. 3 and 4 is a superbly tangled mass of iron drainpipes.

On a weekday, look in briefly at the fourth window on the right, counting from the entrance to the courtyard (bearing in mind that this belongs to a private office of Berry Bros.). Still on the walls of the little room is the original paneling, and above the fireplace are antique port bottles, arranged to show the development of their shapes. The earlier bottles are bulbous with long necks; the modern cylindrical shape emerged around 1760. (It was discovered that port improved with long keeping in the bottle; cylindrical bottles could easily be kept stacked on their sides while the bulbous type could not.)

For the weekend, folding wooden shutters (instead of curtains or blinds) are drawn across the windows inside. Shutters like this were made well into the nineteenth century and are now a valued feature of an old building. They gave security in a way that curtains obviously didn't. They also provided better insulation and lasted far longer. Underneath Pickering Place is part of the cellars of Berry Bros. (Other cellars of the firm stretch below St. James's Street.) In this section of the cellars, Napoleon III is believed to have plotted his return to France during his exile in the 1840s.

Before going to St. James's Palace, the last area of the walk, have a look at the only surviving low alley in the neighborhood. To reach it, go back down the passage into St. James's Street, turn right, and right again at the first corner, into King Street. Thirty yards along King Street on the right is an entry under an archway with its own gaslight. This is **Crown Passage**, an island of working-class life and unpretentious businesses. Along it you will find several sandwich bars, the kind of place that visitors seldom use but is known by local office workers for some of the best values in town. At the far end is a pub, **The Red Lion**, with pleasant models of lions' heads above the first story. (There are many pubs with the same names in London and elsewhere.) The flat front of the upper stories suggests that the building has been here since the early nineteenth century or before.

Crown Passage has existed in something like its present form since at least the 1790s, when at the end adjoining King Street there was a "rookery" (a stronghold of slum-dwellers and criminals who "rooked"—cheated—people). There were similar slums and alleys to the east, the direction away from St. James's Street. Part of this area was described in the mid-nineteenth century as a "low den of infamy." Haymarket, the teeming headquarters of Victorian prostitution, was less than half a mile away to the northeast.

Leaving Crown Passage by the far end, you'll come out into **Pall Mall**. This street is dominated now by ponderous Victorian buildings containing gentlemen's clubs. In the seventeenth century it was a far quieter place, and got its name from a game played here by royalty with a wooden ball ("pell" or "pall") and mallet ("mell" or

Crown Passage

"mall"). King James I may have introduced the game to England in 1603 or soon afterwards; he advised his short-lived son Henry to become fairly good at it: "The exercises that I would have you to use (although but moderately, not making a craft of them) are running, leaping, wrestling, fencing, archery, pall mall. . . ." Expertise was to be avoided, because it was thought by aristocrats to be vulgar—the mark of one who had to earn a living.

The poet and flatterer Edmund Waller, who wrote the lines about Charles II's snow well, also produced some excited verse about Charles's skill at pall mall. According to Waller, a ball struck by the King went like a shot from a culverin (a long cannon):

> *Here a well-polished mall gives us the joy*
> *To see our prince his matchless force employ . . .*
> *No sooner has he touched the flying ball,*
> *But 'tis already more than half the mall,*
> *And such a fury from his arm has got*
> *As from a smoking culverin 'twere shot.*

Cross Pall Mall and go to the right (into Cleveland Row), to the great gate-house tower of **St. James's Palace**. The tower is of faded red brick, has four stories, and stands astride a pair of massive and battered wooden gates. At each corner are octagonal turrets, crowned with battlements. This is the grandest part of the palace to have survived from the time of Henry VIII. On each side of the wooden gates is a small doorway; look closely at the one on the left, and in its top right corner you can just make out worn figures cut in the stone. There is a crown and below it a Tudor rose. This badge was formed by combining the rival red and white roses, emblems of the great warring families of fifteenth-century England— the houses of Lancaster and York. Henry VIII was the son of a victorious Lancastrian father, Henry Tudor (Henry VII), but his mother—Elizabeth of York—was from the other side. The Tudor rose, when painted, shows a red rose encircling a white.

Close to you is a sentry box, normally manned by a soldier from one of the elite Guards regiments. The guardsmen are often recruited for their powerful physiques. Their officers, however, are chosen partly for their social background; it's understood that an officer without a private income would be unlikely to afford the large informal expenses of life in the Guards. The sentries here are guardsmen, not officers; their job, as well as being decorative, is to protect the members of the Royal Family who live in, or close to, St. James's Palace.

A few yards past the gate house is a huge window: this belongs to the Chapel Royal, the setting for some passionate and some comical events, as we shall see shortly. On the sidewalk are the standards of gas lamps put up in the 1820s. Near their base they have the insignia of King George IV, who reigned from 1820 to 1830. The first public gaslights in London were set up in 1807, near here in Pall Mall. George Cruikshank greeted them with a cartoon showing passersby retching from the gas, a bird dropping dead from the sky, and a gassed cat slithering helplessly down a roof.

This wing of St. James's Palace was fitted out in 1795 to receive an unfortunate royal bride, Caroline of Brunswick. Her fiancé was the prince who later became George IV. Sadly for her, George was already married, secretly, to a woman named Maria Fitzherbert. Maria was a Catholic, and if George had married her publicly he would have lost his claim to the throne; even today the heir to the throne is not allowed to marry a Catholic. George was intermittently attached to Maria for many years but ran very heavily into debt; by 1794 he owed over £600,000. An open, official marriage with someone else would help to overcome this, because Parliament would then vote George an increased allowance to meet his new marital responsibilities. So Caroline, George's cousin, was summoned from Germany.

When she arrived in London, George was taken aback by the appearance of the ample, cheerful, and dark young woman. When they met, his first words were not to her but to an attendant: "I am not well. Pray get me a glass of brandy." Caroline was given as her close companion Lady Jersey, George's current mistress and a willing spy, who relayed parts of Caroline's letters to George's mother. At the wedding in the Chapel Royal, the Archbishop of Canterbury paused deliberately when asking whether anyone knew of an impediment to the marriage. But no one spoke, and George acquired a second wife.

The intimacy of the royal couple did not last long, though a daughter resulted—Charlotte, whose sad death we noted earlier in the walk. In January 1796, just three days after Charlotte was born, her father decided on suicide and drew up a romantic, self-dramatizing will leaving an insulting sum—one shilling—to Charlotte's mother. The rest of the estate, George wrote, was to go to "Maria Fitzherbert, my wife, the wife of my heart and soul . . . my true and real wife, and who is dearer to me, even millions of times dearer to me, than that life I am now going to resign." George directed that after his death a miniature portrait of Maria was to be "placed right upon my heart." When Maria herself came to die, her coffin was to be placed next to his, the adjoining sides removed and the coffins then soldered together.

After the excitement of writing this, George decided instead to live. He and Caroline drifted further apart, and both found comfort elsewhere. Many years later, in 1820, George formally became King, and Caroline returned from abroad to claim her position as Queen of England. George tried to disown her and had her physically shut out of his Coronation in Westminster Abbey. He also tried to obtain a divorce, thus creating one of the ripest scandals in English history. We shall come to it on the next walk.

Continue along the wall of the palace until you reach the first entrance on the left. Just before turning in, notice the intricate spray of ironwork on the second-story balcony of the house opposite. Inside the palace, in a yard on the right, is a covered walkway, built as part of the royal stables in the 1660s. An important character in this Stable Yard was the royal rat-killer; in 1741 his name was John Gower. His job was highly respected ("an honourable office")—worth £100 a year, a considerable sum. A royal document describes Mr. Gower's handsome coat, which had rats embroidered on the sleeves:

> Received from His Majesty's Great Wardrobe Office a crimson cloth coat lined with blue serge, guarded [edged] with blue velvet and embroidery, richly on back and breast, with His Majesty's letters and crowns, and on the arms with rats and wheatsheaf, being a livery for Mr. John Gower, Rat-Killer in Ordinary to His Majesty.

Another smartly dressed official in the eighteenth century was the herb-strewer, whose job was to perfume the palace: "To Alice Bell, Herb-Strewer to his Majesty, two yards of scarlet cloth for a livery for the year 1716."

On the far side of Stable Yard is a tall, imposing stone building, **Lancaster House**. This was begun in 1825 on the orders of George IV's brother, the Duke of York. The Duke expected to become King on his brother's death, and, in spite of massive debts, was eager to have a grand residence befitting his status. But he died in 1827, three years before his brother, and the unfinished building passed into the hands of his creditors. In this century Lancaster House was given to the nation. Visits are therefore permitted, except during government functions, when the house is sealed off by security men.

The large white building a few yards away across the road from Lancaster House is **Clarence House**, for many years the residence of Queen Elizabeth, the Queen Mother—the widow of the wartime king, George VI, and perhaps the most popular member of the Royal Family in recent times. This house, too, was built to the order of one of George III's sons, William, Duke of Clarence, later William IV. The architect was John Nash, designer of slightly shoddy masterpieces. (More distinguished work of his can be seen a few hundred yards from here, at the far end of The Mall, in Carlton House Terrace, a great white cliff of slender aristocratic houses.)

Unfortunately, regular public access to **Ambassador's Court** was ended in 1980, for undisclosed reasons of "security." Standing at the entrance, though, you can still see on the far side of the court the wall of the **Chapel Royal.** Inside the chapel, in January 1649, King Charles I attended service on the morning of his execution. Defeated in the Civil War by the forces of Parliament, he had at first been spared. But when he raised more forces to reopen the war, the parliamentary chief, Oliver Cromwell, lost patience and said that to have any further dealings with him was "to meddle with an accursed thing." Charles was put on trial; he refused to recognize the court and was sentenced to death. His dignity on the scaffold is a favorite theme of sentimental writers in England, being easier to dramatize than the deaths of countless ordinary soldiers in the Civil Wars. According to one of his attendants, Charles asked for an extra shirt on the January morning, not wishing to shiver and seem afraid. After reaching the scaffold in Whitehall, he made some grave utterances, as the ax lay ready in his view. Twice he broke off in alarm when spectators got close to the ax, calling out in fear that they would blunt it and make his death more painful: "Hurt not the ax that may hurt me"; "Take heed of the ax, pray take heed of the ax!" In the event, only one stroke of it was needed.

Eleven years later the dead King's son, Charles II, regained the throne and began to spend more relaxed hours in the Chapel Royal. The Republicans had been religious enthusiasts; Charles II and his court were the opposite. One preacher here, Dr. South, noticed that during a sermon all the congregation, including King Charles, was asleep. South stopped, changed his tone and called out to one of the sleepers, the powerful Lord Lauderdale:

"My Lord, I am sorry to interrupt your repose, but I must beg you will not snore so loud, lest you awaken His Majesty."

At the end of Charles II's life, a courtier with puritanical leanings, John Evelyn, was shocked by the way Sunday was spent at St. James's Palace:

> I am never to forget the inexpressible luxury, and profaneness, gaming and all dissolution, and as it were total forgetfulness of God (it being Sunday evening) which this day sennight [a week ago] I was witness of; the King, sitting and toying with his concubines Portsmouth, Cleveland and Mazarine etc., a French boy singing love songs in that glorious gallery, whilst about twenty of the great courtiers and other dissolute persons were [playing] at basset round a large table, a bank of at least 2,000 in gold before them.

"Six days after," Evelyn noted with satisfaction, "all was in the dust." King Charles II was dead.

Fifteen years later, in 1700, the Chapel Royal had become a place for fashionable people to show off and flirt—much like St. James's Church in Piccadilly. A certain Bishop Burnet disapproved and complained to Princess Anne (niece of the late Charles II) about the amorous "ogling and sighing" that went on in the chapel. He wanted the wooden pews to be built up, so that the worshippers would no longer be able to look at each other. He got his way, and a satirical poem appeared, hinting that the Bishop had simply been anxious to get the pretty women to gaze at him instead. In the poem the Bishop is "quoted" as complaining to the Princess about the flirtation in chapel, and then as saying:

> *These practices, Madam, my preaching disgrace;*
> *Shall Laymen enjoy the just rights of my place?*
> *Then all may lament my condition so hard,*

Who thrash in the pulpit without a reward.
 Therefore, pray condescend
 Such disorders to end,
And to the ripe vineyards the labourers send,
To build up the seats that the beauties may see
The face of no brawling pretender but me.
The Princess, by the man's importunity pressed,
Though she laughed at his reasons, allowed his request:
And now Britain's nymphs, in a Protestant reign,
Are locked up at prayers like the virgins in Spain.

Keeping Clarence House on your left, go through the great iron gates into The Mall. When you reach it, look back over the wall to the left, to the late-seventeenth-century section of St. James's Palace which joins Clarence House and runs parallel to The Mall. Near the east (right) end of this wing is the room where a son was born in 1688 to King James II, the Catholic brother of Charles II. Many Protestants were eager for James to be succeeded by one of his grown-up daughters, Mary or Anne, who were Protestants. But when James had a son by Mary of Modena, his second wife, an Italian Catholic, it seemed that Catholic rule might become permanent. So, as a result of wishful thinking or pure lying, many people were persuaded that the baby was not the child of James and Mary but had been smuggled into Mary's chamber in a warming pan. According to different versions, Mary had either miscarried or not been pregnant at all. Smuggling in the child at the right time would certainly have been difficult. There were sixty-seven people present in Mary's bedchamber, many of them high officials of state checking that the birth was indeed genuine. One critic of the story wrote that

the warming pan is no feasible project, unless you break the back of the child to put it in; moreover, as this is supposed to be a tender infant, just reeking and wet from its mother's womb, in that tender state it would either have cried out in the passage, or have been still and dead, and in the variety of motions of tossing it up and down, it would have been a perfect jelly.

But the rumor remained lively and encouraged the Protestant forces which ejected King James from England a few months later. The baby grew up to be known as "The Pretender." Based in France, he inspired the Scottish Rebellion of 1715. His son, "Bonnie Prince Charlie" (also called "The Young Pretender"), led the Scottish uprising of 1745.

Turn left into The Mall, and turn left again at the next corner into Marlborough Road. About 100 yards along is an opening into another section of St. James's Palace, **Friary Court**. A brick balcony with ornamental battlements runs the length of the far side. Here, on the morning after the death of a monarch, the successor is proclaimed to the crowds below. One of the most anxiously awaited of all royal proclamations occurred on the balcony in 1837. That story will end the walk.

In the 1830s royalty had reached a crisis. There had not been a profoundly impressive monarch for centuries, since the death of Queen Elizabeth in 1603. Of the most recent kings George III had been mad (in his last years he thought he was an animal in Noah's Ark), George IV had been wildly scandalous, and William IV ("Silly Billy") was little better. Next in line was the promising schoolgirl Princess Victoria—unless she were to die. But many were afraid that she would die, because the person who stood to benefit, the second in line of succession, was the reckless and vicious Duke of Cumberland.

Cumberland's record was dreadful, and when he appeared in the streets he was usually hissed. As a politician he once bribed men to produce an anti-Catholic demonstration and had been caught using bribery at a parliamentary election. In private life he had scandalized a French nunnery by making eyes at the nuns and trying to kiss the abbess. On another occasion his valet, a Corsican named Sellis, had attacked him and inflicted serious wounds; it was said that Sellis had found Cumberland in bed with his wife. Sellis was found shortly afterwards with his throat cut, probably a suicide. Cumberland's name was later linked with that of a Lady Graves; her husband too was found with his throat cut. Cumberland, in middle age, also tried to rape the wife of the Lord Chancellor in her own home. This was the man who stood to become King of England if Victoria were to die, and whose unpopularity could perhaps have brought monarchy to an end. Rumors that he wished to kill Victoria were so powerful that Cumberland had to issue a discreet denial; he stated in the House of Lords that he was willing to shed his last drop of blood for "that innocent person" Victoria. But in 1837 he inherited the throne of the little German kingdom of Hanover and was obliged to go. He tried to delay his departure from England, only to be told by the Duke of Wellington, "Go—before you are pelted out!" Reluctantly, Cumberland went.

So it was that on June 21, 1837, Victoria, freed from the shadow of her sinister uncle, stood at the balcony here to be proclaimed Queen at the age of eighteen. She looked pale and anxious and, out of respect for the dead William IV, was dressed "in deep mourning, with a white tippet [cape], white cuffs and a border of white lace under a small black bonnet, which was placed far back upon her head, exhibiting her light hair in front simply parted over the forehead." After blasts from trumpets and cannons and intense cheering from the crowd below the balcony, Victoria was overcome. She turned to her mother and wept.

In her reign Victoria was often generous and enlightened, especially behind the scenes. She collaborated with Florence Nightingale to stop the custom of reducing soldiers' pay when they fell sick. She insisted that her Indian subjects not be treated arrogantly by British administrators. In private life, she intervened to help rehabilitate Mary Ann Evans (the brilliant novelist George Eliot) after she had been partly ostracized for living with a (technically) married man. Victoria made mistakes, but her general decency was obvious. She succeeded in largely abolishing the memory of her wicked Hanoverian predecessors. The present Royal Family still profits from the respect which she earned.

Walk · 4

London's Latin Quarter

CHELSEA

WALK 4: Chelsea

FULHAM RD.

SYDNEY ST.

MARKHAM SQUARE

MARKHAM ST.

SMITH

CHELSEA

RADNOR WK.

SMITH TER

MANOR ST.

FLOOD ST.

OLD CHURCH ST.

KING'S RD.

OAKLEY ST.

BEAUFORT ST.

UPPER CHEYNE ROW

CHEYNE GDNS.

JUSTICE WK.

LAWRENCE ST.

CHEYNE ROW

CHEYNE MEWS

Carlyle's House

CHEYNE WK.

C

CHEYNE

Chelsea Old Church

ALBERT BRIDGE

River Thames

BATTERSEA BRIDGE

Royal Court Theatre
⬛ Royal Court Theatre
⊖ SLOANE SQUARE

SLOANE ST.
CLIVEDEN PL.
SLOANE SQ.
SLOANE GDNS.
BOURNE ST.
KING'S RD.
LOWER SLOANE ST.
PIMLICO RD.
CHELTENHAM TER.
Duke of York's Hdqtrs.
WALPOLE ST.
ROYAL AVE.
WELLINGTON SQ.
ST.
WOODFALL ST.
FRANKLIN'S ROW
ST. LEONARD'S TER.
BURTON'S CT.
ROYAL HOSPITAL RD.
CHELSEA BRIDGE RD.
RANELAGH GARDENS
DURHAM PL.
ORMONDE GATE
TITE
ST.
PARADISE WK.
National Army Museum
Royal Hospital
SWAN WK.
DILKE ST.
Physic Garden
ELSEA EMBANKMENT
CHELSEA BRIDGE
River Thames
BATTERSEA PARK

Starting Point: Sloane Square tube station
Buses: 11, 19, 22, 137

For Londoners, "Chelsea" means above all the King's Road, a long, fashionable, crowded street just to the west of central London and a few hundred yards north of the Thames. Here the fashion designer Mary Quant opened her first shop in 1955. Imitators soon appeared, and the King's Road became a main artery of Swinging London in the 1960s. Quant's shop is now gone, but the road has held its magnetism for young people. They come to display their new clothes and poses—so don't be afraid to stare!

Only a few of the younger people on the sidewalk actually live in Chelsea. Housing in the area is wildly expensive. A spacious house in the most favored part of Chelsea is likely to cost around a million pounds. In the 1970s Mick Jagger and Keith Richards lived here; their neighbors included Paul Getty, a duchess, and Mrs. Margaret Thatcher. Most of our walk will be in this residential section, away from the King's Road and close to the river. Here you will find quiet eighteenth-century terraces, some built in a grand sweep to overlook the Thames, others

177

clustered around a little street wide enough only for a single horse-drawn carriage.

Chelsea has been a chic address since the early sixteenth century, when Thomas More built himself a large house near the river. As Henry VIII's Lord Chancellor, More had a set of uniformed boatmen to take him downstream to court. Henry visited More at Chelsea, liked the area, and in 1536, shortly after arranging More's execution, unsentimentally began to build himself a home here. King Henry's manor house became the residence of two of his six queens. Many years later, its last occupant was Sir Hans Sloane, an eighteenth-century society physician. Sloane demolished More's nearby house, but to his credit arranged for the building of an elegant riverside terrace, Cheyne (pronounced "chainy") Walk. Sloane also saved the Physic Garden, a walled sanctuary for rare and medicinal plants—which, like Cheyne Walk, still survives. On Sloane's death in 1753, much of his Chelsea estate passed to his daughter, Elizabeth. She married an aristocrat named Cadogan, and the Cadogan family have remained landlords here to the present day.

In the nineteenth century Chelsea had a colony of famous writers and artists, British, Irish, and American. George Eliot, the novelist, lived on Cheyne Walk. Oscar Wilde, the exotic bisexual playwright, spent his greatest years nearby in Tite Street. In the same street the artist James McNeill Whistler built his ideal house, only to lose it within months because of a disastrous lawsuit. John Singer Sargent painted his lavish portraits of society ladies in a neighboring studio. Oscar Wilde teased one of them from his doorstep as she passed on her way to a sitting with Sargent—dressed as Lady Macbeth.

One house especially symbolizes Chelsea's bohemian past: the riverside home of Dante Gabriel Rossetti, the mid-Victorian painter and poet. Here numerous models and mistresses drifted in and out, helping themselves to large supplies of money stuffed handily into a drawer. The place was a ménage inside and a menagerie outside with Rossetti's expensive and impractical zoo. Especially lovable, as we shall see, were the pet armadillos—skillful little miners with no sense of property boundaries. Rossetti's peacocks, which flew screeching up into the neighbors' trees, caused serious complaints; so the Cadogan estate wrote, and still writes, a special clause into its leases that strictly forbids the keeping of peacocks.

Leave Sloane Square tube station and go a few steps to the right, to the entrance of the **Royal Court Theatre**. The sidewalk here is a favorite spot for social display, especially on summer evenings when theatergoers are arriving. In the 1950s the Royal Court added to Chelsea's bohemian reputation by launching the play *Look Back in Anger*, one of the first signs of the revolt against English postwar dullness and conservatism. The playwright, John Osborne, published a famous letter explaining why he hated England, and completed the act by emigrating. He returned not long afterwards, having secured his reputation as an Angry Young Man, and wrote the excellent screenplay for the film *Tom Jones*.

In a moment you'll be leaving Sloane Square by an exit on its far side, almost directly opposite the tube station. But look first at **Sloane Street**, which leaves the square to the right, just 20 yards beyond the theater. This spot is now entirely urban, and it is hard to imagine that the road here was once desolate at night and dreaded by travelers from London. A few yards down that road to the right was Bloody Bridge, over a stream called the Westbourne, and people who had to cross it made attractive targets for highwaymen. Robbery was so common in the eighteenth century that some travelers used to carry two purses—one, well hidden, containing most of their money and another one to be surrendered to highwaymen. The Westbourne, like other London streams, now runs underground to the Thames; at Sloane Square tube station it crosses the railway tracks in a great iron case.

Walk around Sloane Square to the far side. Of the

two exits there, take the one on the left, **King's Road**. You will then have on your right the large and respected general store Peter Jones.

Fifty yards beyond Peter Jones, on the left, are hefty iron railings; go almost to the end of them, then look through at the stylish classical building, with columns and portico, that overlooks a large lawn. The building, called the **Duke of York's Headquarters**, was begun in 1801 as a school for the children of soldiers. Children still play on the lawn, but the buildings nearby are now barracks. The school was founded by the Duke of York— George III's second son—who was in some ways an effective military reformer. During the Napoleonic Wars he tried to abolish the old practice of buying military commissions for prestige or to gain access to valuable military stores. Utterly unsuitable people had become officers in this way, and the Duke called for the resignations of all colonels under the age of twenty and captains under the age of twelve. His reforming, however, was interrupted in 1809, when it emerged that his own mistress had been selling commissions. The Duke was forced to resign in disgrace.

Pass Cheltenham Terrace, the next turn on the left; a few steps farther, on the right-hand side of King's Road, the row of Chelsea boutiques begins. Look above the modernized and rather brash shop fronts and you will see the decayed flat façades of early-nineteenth-century houses. Farther along King's Road, the second opening on the left is the impressive Royal Avenue. Before turning into it, walk for another 100 yards along King's Road to where Markham Square opens on the right. The building at the corner of the square, **no. 138** King's Road, is where Mary Quant first went into business with a shop called Bazaar. When Quant, a young ex-student, and her backers converted the building into a shop, their enterprise was very nearly ruined at the outset. Planning permission for the architectural changes had not been obtained, and a local government official ordered Quant and her friends to restore the building to its original shape—at their own expense. The backers and Quant herself (in tears) besieged the official and in the end obtained the permission they wanted.

The shop began purely as a retail venture, with an associated restaurant in the basement. (Guests at the restaurant included Brigitte Bardot. When she appeared, service came to a standstill; the male waiters clustered around—to gaze at the beautiful man who accompanied her.) Mary Quant began designing when she found that she couldn't get from wholesalers the unusual designs she wanted. She later wrote a breathless and delightful book, *Quant by Quant*, about the chaotic but highly successful early days of her business. Many of her dress patterns were eaten by Siamese cats: "It took me some time to discover that the tissue paper used to make these patterns is manufactured from some by-product of fish bones." The name Bazaar was at the time zany and original, and the window displays were also meant to surprise. Once, when the theme was vacation clothes, the window was filled with milk bottles to suggest a hasty holiday departure. Mary Quant did her market research by listening secretly to what passersby had to say about her displays through a ventilator in the shop wall.

Quant had more influence on the fashions of the sixties than perhaps anyone else in the world. Among her new ideas was the use for fashion of the shiny fabric polyvinylchloride. This became standard dress even for radicals who supposedly turned their backs on fashion. Many of the demonstrating anarchists and Marxists of the late sixties were, without knowing it, dressed for "battle" in the styles of Mary Quant.

Now go back along King's Road to **Royal Avenue**, a grand set of late Georgian terraces that face each other across lines of trees. Walk along the right-hand side of the avenue, where you will see several fine old lights above the doors; look at the short, vertical metal bars set into the glass over the doors of **nos. 14, 16**, and **22**. Near

Window shopping, King's Road

Skinheads, King's Road

the far end, at **no. 48**, the second-story window has an extremely intricate set of wooden shutters behind it. Right at the end of the avenue, the road's original purpose becomes clear. By looking straight ahead, through the ornamental iron gates, you can see in the distance the Royal

Hospital, built in the 1680s and 1690s as a home for soldiers. (A Latin inscription in the building says that it was designed for men "broken by war and old age.") Royal Avenue was meant to be part of a grand route joining the hospital and a palace at Kensington, but when its promoter, Charles II, died, the scheme was dropped.

By looking between the lines of trees that run towards the hospital, you can make out the cupola on its roof and also the rounded, baroque windows favored by its architect, Christopher Wren. Although still in use, the building has the feeling of a grand and rather bleak monument, and so it isn't on our route. (It can be visited in the afternoons, and if you'd like to be guided around the fine chapel and dining hall, one of the old soldiers will oblige eagerly. Payment is expected.) You may already have seen some of the building's residents wearing their uniform frock-coats and with the initials of the Royal Hospital on their caps. They are usually called "Chelsea pensioners": many have distinguished war records, and some have an envied ability to attract gifts of beer in local pubs. Nowadays almost all are elderly, but in earlier times younger men were admitted. In 1765 two of the pensioners attacked and murdered a traveler on the edge of Chelsea; evidently they weren't yet "broken by war and old age." They were caught and executed, and for months afterwards their tarred bodies hung twisting in the wind, as a macabre deterrent.

The road at the end of Royal Avenue is **St. Leonard's Terrace**; turn left for a moment, and go along to the next corner on the left (Walpole Street). **No. 7** St. Leonard's Terrace in the late 1970s was the home of Laurence Olivier. In front of the house notice the artfully bulging railings of the balconies. Then retrace your steps along St. Leonard's Terrace back to Royal Avenue, and go about 100 yards farther. **No. 18** St. Leonard's Terrace has a dignified plain frontage, with a metal canopy over the door and an ancient boot scraper outside it that dates from the days of muddy streets. Low railings with spikes prevent illegal access to the basement; their lowness leads you to guess that they were installed when people were, on average, a few inches shorter than they are today.

In the late nineteenth century this was the home of Bram Stoker, the tall and handsome Irish actor and novelist who invented Count Dracula. Stoker's novel *Dracula* was published in 1897, when he was living here. There was a historical Dracula, a certain Vlad Drakul who ruled Wallachia (now part of Rumania) in the fifteenth century and was famous for impaling his enemies on stakes. But it was Stoker who turned Dracula into a coffin-dwelling bloodsucker, with glamorous "undead" female followers. His gothic novel, with its exaggerated horror and its interest in medieval ruins, shows signs of having been written in a great hurry. But it's still worth reading, especially the passage in which the count's young English victim, detained in Castle Dracula, first realizes that there is something very wrong about his host:

> The window at which I stood was tall and deep, stone mullioned, and though weather worn, was still complete; . . . I drew back behind the stonework, and looked carefully out.
>
> What I saw was the Count's head coming out from the window below. I did not see the face. . . . I was at first interested and somewhat amused . . . but my very feelings changed to repulsion and terror when I saw the whole man slowly emerge from the window and begin to crawl down the castle wall over that dreadful abyss, *face down*, with his cloak spread out around him like great wings. . . . I saw the fingers and toes grasp the corners of the stones, worn clear of the mortar by the stress of years, and by thus using every projection and inequality move downwards with considerable speed, just as a lizard moves along a wall.

It is sad, perhaps, that Stoker himself did not realize the stage potential of his creation. The first serious stage pro-

duction of *Dracula* was in 1924, twelve years after Stoker's death. When the show reached the West End, a nurse had to be employed to deal with the numerous people in the audience who fainted: seven was average for an evening; the maximum was twenty-nine. One report said of the people who fainted: "strangely enough, they were generally men." (All this made excellent publicity, and the show soon opened in New York with the leading role played by a little-known Hungarian who went on to become the definitive ghoul—Bela Lugosi. Lugosi also played in the superb 1931 Universal film *Dracula*. In the film, the monster at one point is climbing the stairs of his castle, passing through cobwebs which remain, of course, unbroken. Suddenly the howling of wolves is heard through a window—she-vampires calling to the Master. Dracula turns, his great cloak swirling around him, and his voice echoes down the stone staircase, "Listen to them—children of the night. What *music* they make.")

Next door to Stoker's house, at **no. 19**, the most beautiful section of St. Leonard's Terrace begins. Creeping plants reach high up the fronts of the elegant eighteenth-century houses, which look out over fields toward the Royal Hospital. Between **nos. 21** and **22** are delicate iron railings. **Nos. 26–30** are the oldest houses in the row, dating from the mid-eighteenth century. **No. 26** has an intricately carved wooden door frame, like its neighbors. Above the door is a light with strips of metal that intersect to form pointed, Gothic arches.

Just beyond these houses, at the intersection with Smith Street, is a mailbox ("pillar box") from Stoker's day. It is about five feet high, hexagonal in design, and has a petal motif on the top. It bears the insignia of Queen Victoria (VR—Victoria Regina). Above the narrow slit for letters is the royal badge of lion and unicorn. Today Victorian pillar boxes of this type are rare survivors. In most areas they have long since been removed, probably because of the narrowness of the slit. But in Chelsea style is more likely to be put before convenience, and the res-

idents are powerful enough to have their views respected by the Post Office.

Turn right, into **Smith Street,** for a moment. Thirty yards along, on the left, is the entry to **Smith Terrace,** a delightful crescent of small Georgian houses. Originally built for fairly humble residents, the terrace has now been revamped and painted in pastel shades.

Go back to Smith Street and turn right. There will now be a walk of a few hundred yards which will bring you into Old Chelsea's most bohemian quarter. Return to the corner with the Victorian pillar box, and carry on straight ahead, passing a terrace on the right called Durham Place and then its continuation, Ormonde Gate. Where this street ends—at the junction with Royal Hospital Road—turn right and then into the first street on the left, **Tite Street.** This street has far more history, and chic, than its rather ordinary-looking buildings and empty sidewalks might suggest. On the right of the street is a tall terrace of red-brick Victorian houses with balconies and bow fronts. Here at **no. 34** (formerly no. 16) was the home of Oscar Wilde.

Wilde, a young playwright from Dublin, moved here shortly after his marriage, in 1884, to Constance Lloyd, "a beautiful girl" (in Wilde's words), "a grave, slight, violet-eyed little Artemis, with great coils of heavy brown hair which make her flower-like head droop like a blossom." They had two children soon afterwards. Helped by Constance's money, Wilde turned the interior of the house into an aesthete's paradise. The room just to the right of the front door was a study, with walls of buttercup yellow set off with red lacquer. The dining room was decorated in shades of white, with "each table a sonnet in ivory, and the main table . . . a masterpiece in pearl." Wilde's house was to be "a tower of ivory," with unpleasantness utterly excluded.

By the 1890s Wilde's plays were earning him a great deal of money, and he spent much of it on boys and young men, among them Lord Alfred Douglas. In 1895 unpleasantness arrived here at Wilde's door, in the shape of Douglas's father, the Marquess of Queensberry. Queensberry, a member of a famous sporting family, was appalled by his son's homosexual behavior and had come to remonstrate with Wilde. He was, however, firmly invited to leave, with Wilde telling his servant, so that the Marquess could hear, never again to let in "the most infamous brute in London." Queensberry retaliated by going to Wilde's club and leaving a note addressed to "Oscar Wilde posing as a somdomite" (a misspelling which consequently became famous). Wilde was greatly upset, exclaiming that "the tower of ivory is assailed by the foul thing." He prosecuted the Marquess for libel, lost, and caused so much evidence to emerge that he himself became liable for prosecution as a homosexual. The police gave him time to flee the country, perhaps following orders from on high (Wilde had some important political connections). But instead he sat drinking with Lord Alfred Douglas until he was arrested. He was given two years' imprisonment and later wrote *The Ballad of Reading Gaol* about his experiences. Popular with prisoners and warders, he used to help the warders prepare their entries for newspaper literary competitions. The staff of Reading prison suddenly found themselves winning substantial prizes, including a tea service and a grand piano.

Even after his disgrace, some of Wilde's work remained popular. His play *The Importance of Being Earnest* kept on running (though with the author's name removed from all the advertisements). For this play Wilde invented an upper-class monster, Lady Bracknell, a character still well remembered in England. When a young man wishes to marry her daughter, Lady Bracknell questions him about his social origins and respectability, and explodes on being told that he doesn't know his origins because he was found as a baby in a handbag in a station cloakroom. She informs the young man that discovery in a handbag can hardly be regarded as a secure basis for a career in society, adding, "You can hardly imagine that I and Lord Bracknell would dream of allowing our only daughter—a girl brought up with the utmost care—to marry into a cloakroom, and form an alliance with a parcel."

Wilde was master of the shrewd and memorable overstatement: "Work is the curse of the drinking classes," "Men become old but they never become good," "The very essence of romance is uncertainty," and "Hard work is simply the refuge of people who have nothing whatever to do." Even during his trial he found time to make phrases: "All is well," he said; "the working classes are with me—to a boy."

Soon after Wilde's imprisonment, Queensberry arranged to have him driven into bankruptcy. The contents of "the house beautiful" here were virtually looted, and Wilde's wife and children were driven out. Wilde suffered, after his release, as an impoverished exile. In different ways, so did his wife. One of their young sons summed up the position well, toward the end of their stay in Tite Street. Wilde had scolded him for being a naughty boy and for making mother cry; the young Wilde replied that Oscar was a "naughty Papa," who "did not come home till the early morning and made mother cry far more."

A hundred yards farther down Tite Street, on the left, is a small irregular block with very large windows. It contained studios in Chelsea's artistic heyday. In the first section **(no. 31)** John Singer Sargent worked for many years; he eventually died here in 1925. American by parentage and European by upbringing, Sargent produced many imposing oil paintings of wealthy young women, usually wearing extravagantly beautiful dresses. He may have performed the role of earlier portraitists in the days before photography—helping to attract suitable husbands for young ladies with dowries. Highly successful in its day, Sargent's work is still respected on both sides of the Atlantic.

Next door, at **no. 33**, the Welsh portraitist Augustus

John had a studio in the years around 1950. A charismatic figure, bearded and with loose-fitting clothes, John attracted and occasionally mistreated numerous women. Among his best-remembered works today is a sketch of T. E. Lawrence in Arab headdress, looking spiritual and decisive.

Just beyond this block, on the same side of the street, is **no. 35**. Until the late 1970s this belonged to a gentleman named the Honorable Colin Tennant, the owner of the Caribbean holiday island of Mustique. Among his guests on the island have been Princess Margaret and her friend Roddy Llewellyn. When Tennant decided to sell this house, it was advertised at £500,000. A few weeks later, I was pointing out the place to some friends when a grand Chelsea lady came past. "That," she informed us, "has just been sold to the Arabs for half a million pounds," and swept away. Notice: the Arabs. People in West London, where many Arabs have recently bought houses, often get conspiracy-minded.

A more famous house once stood on this site, the "white house" built in the 1870s for the admired American painter James McNeill Whistler, by the architect E. W. Godwin. Whistler loved Chelsea and produced many impressionistic paintings of the Thames in this area. His house in Tite Street, built of white brick and green slate, was to be home, studio and school. But while the house was being built, a painting of Whistler's—*The Falling Rocket, a Nocturne in Black and Gold*—was attacked in print by the art critic John Ruskin. Ruskin, objecting to the impressionism and lack of precise detail, claimed that Whistler was impudently asking 200 guineas (£210) for "flinging a pot of paint in the public's face." Whistler sued for libel, won his case, was awarded one farthing—a quarter of a penny—in damages, and ordered to pay his own enormous legal costs. He was, temporarily, ruined. He tried to persuade creditors to accept his own paintings instead of cash (which, as it turned out, would have been a wonderful bargain), but the offer was rejected. One creditor wrote back, "It is not a Nocturne in purple or a Symphony in blue and grey that we are after, but an Arrangement in gold and silver." Whistler was forced to sell his beloved house in 1879, before it was completed. Just before leaving, he wrote above the front door, "Except the Lord build the house, they labour in vain that build it. E. W. Godwin built this one."

Opposite is the start of **Dilke Street.** Go along here for a few steps, then turn for a moment into the first opening on the right, **Paradise Walk.** After an unprom- ising first section, this is now a prettily painted terrace of two-storied Georgian cottages with wooden shutters out- side the windows. But in the mid-nineteenth century it was one of London's worst slums, its houses packed with ragged families. Oscar Wilde's "tower of ivory" over- looked the back of this street; he put a screen over his window to block the view.

Come back to Dilke Street, turn right and, a few yards farther, look into the next entrance on the right, **Clover Mews.** (A mews is a terrace, with residential quarters above a first story which was once stables and is now converted into garages. The word *mews* came from the French *muer*, "to molt," and originally meant a place where tame hawks were kept during their periods of molting. The residential part of a mews is usually small, as here.) Notice the rough surface of the street outside, which adds to the antique atmosphere, and the window boxes—*de rigueur* for mews-dwellers.

Turn right into Dilke Street again. A few steps farther and you will come to the end of the street. The road which runs left and right here is **Swan Walk,** one of the most pleasant of Chelsea's quiet places. The name "Swan" came from the (now vanished) Swan Inn, which stood on the old river bank close to where you're standing. The river was pushed back to its present banks when the Chelsea Embankment was built in the early 1870s. Sam- uel Pepys describes paying a visit to this spot at the time of the great plague, and getting a shock:

> By coach to Mrs. Pierce's and with her and (Mrs.)
> Knipp and Mrs. Pierce's boy and girl abroad,
> thinking to have been merry at Chelsea; but being
> come almost to the house by coach near the wa-
> terside, a house alone, I think the Swan, a gentle-
> man walking by called to us to tell us that the
> house was shut up of the sickness. So we with
> great affright turned back . . . and went away (I
> for my part in great disorder).

Pepys mentions how grateful he felt to this gentleman for preventing them from going any closer to the place of infection.

Facing you, on the far side of Swan Walk, is a long wall about eight feet high. Behind it is the private **Physic Garden:** go 50 yards to the right along Swan Walk and you can look in through an iron gate. The garden was first laid out in the 1670s by the apothecaries—herbalists who played an important role in English medicine. Here their precious plants grew; notice on top of the gate the wicked old spikes to prevent intruders. In 1685 the di- arist John Evelyn visited the garden, described the inge- nious system of underground heating in the plant-houses, and noted the tree that produced Jesuits' bark, "which had done such cures in quartans." (Quartan ague was malaria, and Jesuits' bark contained quinine.) Later, in 1722, the apothecaries ran into financial difficulties, and Sir Hans Sloane generously leased them the garden at a fixed low rent. In recognition, they set up a marble statue of Sloane, made by a leading sculptor of the 1730s, Mi- chael Rysbrack. You can see it straight ahead of you through the gate; Sloane is wearing a full-bottomed wig.

In 1732 the garden provided help for a new colony in America, designed for poor debtors and named Geor- gia after the British monarch of the day, George II. A supply of cottonseed was sent from here to Georgia, and from that seed developed the great cotton industry of the American South. Years later, Britain in turn came to rely on imports of cotton from America. During the American Civil War, the blockade of the southern states prevented this cotton from reaching England, with dire results. About a fifth of the English population depended on the cotton industry, and pressure was put on the British government to join the war on the side of the Confederates—which it nearly did. In those days, British naval intervention mattered; the British navy was the largest in the world, and less than fifty years had passed since a British force had won the battle of Bladensburg and burned Washington. However, in 1861 Queen Victoria's husband, Prince Albert, intervened from his deathbed to prevent the British government from sending an inflammatory message to the Union government. If sent, this would probably have brought Britain into the war, and might have altered its result. So the cottonseeds from this garden had some far-reaching effects.

Also in the 1730s the Physic Garden was used by one of the greatest of botanical artists, Elizabeth Blackwell. Until her day, accurate illustrations of herbs were difficult or impossible to find. She made herself an expert through years of studying the plants in this garden and produced a meticulous and beautifully illustrated book entitled *A Curious* (careful) *Herbal*. Part of her long task was to color the printed illustrations by hand. Copies of the book still exist, and under each illustration is written in Latin, "Elizabeth Blackwell drew, engraved, and painted this." The text, compiled by her husband, is less original, but has some interesting entries: "Turnips are accounted very wholesome and nourishing, but somewhat windy. A syrup, made with slices of turnip and brown sugar candy baked in an oven, is commended as a good pectoral, and of great service for coughs and consumptions." Some of Mrs. Blackwell's illustrations show insects associated with the plants. With the garden radish is shown the "Mole Cricket—It lives commonly upon roots, and seldom comes abroad till ye sun is down."

It seems that Elizabeth Blackwell produced this book

to help herself and her husband out of serious debt caused by his failure as a printer. While doing her research, she lived in Swan Walk, probably at no. 4. (The building is still standing, a fine detached Georgian house just across the road.) Mr. Blackwell, however, got into further trouble. He went to work at the court of Sweden, became suspected of plotting, and was sentenced to death. An English newspaper of the time reported that when Blackwell knelt at the block, the executioner told him that he was on the wrong side of it. He replied dryly that the mistake was understandable, since this was the first time he had ever been beheaded. Elizabeth Blackwell survived her husband and was buried in Chelsea Old Church in 1758.

Behind their railings and garden walls, the detached eighteenth-century houses in Swan Walk are three-storied and of faded brick. At **no. 2,** notice the hanging-basket design of the ancient oil lamp over the gate and the fine Corinthian columns of the door frame (best seen from the far side of the road).

Just beyond no. 1 Swan Walk is **Royal Hospital Road** again. Turn left into it, and walk the 150 yards to the junction with Flood Street (on the right). Flood Street itself isn't on the present route, but at the far end of it— no. 19—was in the 1970s the family home of Mrs. Margaret Thatcher.

Also joining Royal Hospital Road here, and forming a corner with Flood Street, is **Cheyne Walk,** one of London's most chic addresses. It is a single line of houses, built to look out over the river and now sheltered from the traffic of Chelsea Embankment by a strip of small trees. The brickwork of the flat, elegant, housefronts has mellowed over the years, and most of the older houses have had a story or two added, but otherwise they remain much as they were built, which was just before 1720, early in the Georgian era. For over a century

Strollers, Chelsea

Cheyne Walk has been the home of people successful in the arts and show business.

A few yards along the walk, at **no. 3,** you can see the wooden shutters behind the first-story windows. In the early 1970s this was the home of Keith Richards, the Rolling Stones guitarist, songwriter and pharmaceutical expert. When the Stones first became known in the early sixties, their manager, Andrew Loog Oldham, tried to publicize mildly unpleasant aspects of the group to give it a distinct image. The Beatles at the time were being sold as cuddly lads from the homely north of England, the sort that any grandmother would be happy to have visiting her teenage granddaughter. So the Stones had to appear as nasties from the decadent English south.

Next door, at **no. 4,** look up at the date molded into the head of the drainpipe: 1718. In the 1860s this was the home of Daniel Maclise, an Irish artist. He was a drinking companion of Charles Dickens and produced both flattering and satirical portraits of him.

Later, in 1880, this was the home for a few weeks of Mary Ann Evans (George Eliot), one of the cleverest— and, to some, one of the most notorious—women of Victorian England. Educated in the unfashionable Midland city of Coventry, she moved to London for work and companionship and became the brains behind an intellectual magazine, the *Westminister Review*. When she began to write fiction, she was extremely nervous about criticism. Even her publisher was not allowed to know her identity, and she chose a male nom de plume to defeat guesswork. She revealed her secret after her work had proved an immediate success and someone in the Midlands had begun to claim that *he* was George Eliot.

George Eliot took pride in the sympathetic but exact description of motives. Especially close to her heart were the characters of Dorothea Brooke and Maggie Tulliver, the young heroines of *Middlemarch* and *The Mill on the Floss.* Dorothea is willing to give away much of her time and fortune to help the poor, but guiltily catches herself wishing that there were slightly more poverty in the neighborhood for her to remedy. Maggie Tulliver as a child is frowned on by her mother for being dark-haired and lively, not blonde and docile like a fashionable girl. But Maggie has her own views about this. She decides to cut off her offending hair, thinking "of the triumph she should have over her mother and her aunts by this very decided course of action: she didn't want her hair to look pretty—that was out of the question—she only wanted people to think her a clever little girl, and not to find fault with her." Her mother despairs of this wayward daughter, but her father has a gleam of hope: perhaps she will grow up clever enough to defeat the local lawyers.

Eliot's feminism is gently acidic, directed against male conceit, against occasionally silly women, and also against the men who encourage them to be so. When a woman in *The Mill on the Floss* says something unusually stupid, her husband smiles happily "with the natural pride of a man who has a buxom wife conspicuously his inferior in intellect." The shallow Sir James Chettam, who tries to court Dorothea in *Middlemarch*, feels himself quite un-threatened by her superior brains. He, after all, is a man, and "a man's mind—what there is of it—has always the advantage of being masculine, as the smallest birch-tree is of a higher kind than the most soaring palm, and even his ignorance is of a sounder quality."

For much of her life, Eliot created scandal by living with the biographer George Lewes. She would have liked to marry him, and she called herself Mrs. Lewes. Lewes, however, was already married. He had treated his wife well, continuing to support her after she had begun to have children by another man, which was before George Eliot came on the scene. But by thus condoning his wife's adultery he had made divorce impossible. Unlike some Victorians, Queen Victoria herself was not put off Eliot's work by the scandal; she was said to be devoted to the novels and eagerly acquired the writer's autograph.

Lewes died in 1878. In the spring of 1880 Eliot married John Cross, a banker more than twenty years her junior. During their honeymoon in Venice, Cross—in a fit of depression—jumped out of a window into a canal. He was pulled out alive, and recovered slowly. He and his wife moved into this house on December 3, 1880. On December 19 she fell ill, and died three days later. Cross wrote, "And I am left alone in this new house we meant to be so happy in."

Next door, **no. 5** Cheyne Walk is now smartly painted and was until recently the home of a Duchess of Devonshire, one of the wealthy Cavendish family. But in the nineteenth century this was the dingy, cobwebbed home of a miser named Neild. Having inherited a fortune from his father, a jeweler, Neild spent much of his life trudging the roads collecting rents from his numerous properties. When he died in 1852, he left half a million pounds—then a colossal fortune—to Queen Victoria. Critics said that his surviving relatives deserved the money more, but Victoria accepted it.

No. 6, adjoining, has only four floors and shows more clearly than its neighbors how Cheyne Walk looked when first built. The front is brick of various colors. Notice, too, the worn stone steps bonded with iron and the iron-studded door to the basement (on the right). On the wall above the main door are two metal fire marks; a resident around 1800 was unusually afraid of losing his property and insured with two fire brigades at once. One mark has the clasped hands of the Amicable Contributors company; the other, showing a lion in a circle, belongs to the British Fire Office. Occasionally a building from this period had even more fire marks; and it was said of King George IV, who liked to decorate himself with numerous medals, that he "looked like an over-insured building." Look at the top of the meandering drainpipes, and you will see the coat of arms of the first residents here in the early eighteenth century, the Danvers family, gentry from the Midlands. When the family left, the place was taken, in 1765, by a Dr. Dominiceti, a Venetian who aimed to cure wealthy patients with vapor baths. After spending huge sums to convert the interior into bath chambers,

Dominiceti found his patients falling away and his debts mounting. He left England, and his creditors, in a hurry.

A few doors along, **no. 10** Cheyne Walk was the home in the 1970s of an artistic couple, well known in Britain: Jane Asher and Gerald Scarfe. Asher is an actress with a successful record on the West End stage. In the 1960s she became famous as a girlfriend of Paul McCartney. Asher looked like an angel, McCartney looked like a choirboy—the nation approved the match, except for McCartney's female fans, of course. Asher also won hearts during a television broadcast when a large spider entered the studio and approached her, unscripted. The gentle-looking lady did not retreat but picked the spider up sympathetically and removed it. Gerald Scarfe is a successful cartoonist, his political work appearing weekly in the *Sunday Times*. He made his name in the sixties, producing venomously distorted caricatures for the satirical magazine *Private Eye*. He has a particular liking for anti-Kremlin cartoons. In 1968, at the time of the Russian invasion of Czechoslovakia and also of the first heart-transplant operations, Scarfe did a cartoon showing Brezhnev and Kosygin, dressed as surgeons, operating on a familiar figure from the Russian past. "Stalin," the caption read, "—New Heart."

Go along to **no. 16** Cheyne Walk, a Georgian house which in 1862 became the home of Dante Gabriel Rossetti. Rossetti belonged to the Pre-Raphaelite group of painters who tried to bring back the intense and detailed style used in early Italian art. He was also a successful poet. When he moved here, Rossetti was recovering from the death of his wife, the beautiful Elizabeth Siddal. He had met her when she was a hatmaker's assistant. She suffered from tuberculosis but sat for many of Rossetti's paintings and was also the subject of several of his love poems. (Many Victorians liked their women "pale and interesting," as Thomas Hardy put it.) The illness was well advanced when she married Rossetti, and she "seemed ready to die daily." When she did die, the distraught and romantic Rossetti had some of his love poems buried with her, wrapped in her lovely hair. Seven years later, when his love for her had dwindled but the value of the poems had not, he made the less romantic gesture of having her dug up to get the manuscripts back. Luckily, she—and they—were quite well preserved.

In this house and its back garden Rossetti kept exotic animals, imported at great expense. Two kangaroos (mother and son) lived in a shed until the young one committed matricide. Later this naughty animal was itself killed, probably by Rossetti's pet raccoon. The artist was especially fond of his wombat, a cuddly Australian marsupial that looks like a large dormouse. Lewis Carroll (Charles Dodgson) visited Rossetti here, and it is thought that the wombat was the original model of the dormouse in the Mad Hatter's Tea Party. One lady who was sitting for a portrait by Rossetti had her straw hat eaten by the wombat. Rossetti was most sympathetic—to the animal: "Ah, poor wombat. It is so indigestible." Most anarchic of all were Rossetti's armadillos, which used to burrow under walls and emerge triumphantly in the neighboring gardens. In a particularly successful breakout, one armadillo dug its way up through a neighbor's kitchen floor, terrifying the cook.

Above the gate of no. 16, half hidden in the decorative ironwork, are the initials of its first resident, Richard Chapman, an apothecary, who leased the place in 1717. A recent resident was Mr. Paul Getty, and you may still see a closed-circuit TV camera by the door. Just across the road, behind the hedge in the public garden, is a bust of Rossetti set up by his friends. He is shown with palette and writing paper to hint at his double artistic role.

When you are a few yards farther along Cheyne Walk, go down the alley (**Cheyne Mews**) that opens to the right and passes close to the front door (and fine fanlight) of no. 24. An ancient sign tells you that "This road is re-

Dante Gabriel Rossetti's house, Cheyne Walk

served for residents and their horses and vehicles." A brief inspection is allowable all the same. The alley passes through a tunnel below no. 24, where there is another sign for those with vehicles: "All drivers of Vehicles are Directed to *Walk* their Horses while passing under this Archway."

Go 60 yards farther down this lane, which is almost as quiet as the country. At the end is a cluster of mews cottages. This was the site of Henry VIII's manor house until its demolition in 1753. Henry gave the house to his last Queen, Catherine Parr, upon their marriage in 1543. The King was by this time exceedingly fat; his surviving fourth wife, Anne of Cleves, who also lived here for a time, said with understandable spite that she did not envy the new Queen her "heavy burden." Catherine continued her residence after Henry's death four years later and was soon being courted by the ambitious Thomas Seymour, Lord High Admiral. She sent him instructions on how to visit her secretly in the garden here very early in the morning. After marrying Catherine, however, Seymour showed an eye for further flirtation with royalty. The young Princess Elizabeth was also living here. Seymour used to enter her bedroom in his nightshirt and try to kiss and cuddle her. Catherine had Elizabeth removed, amid scandalous gossip: the future Virgin Queen angrily denied a rumor that she had been imprisoned in the Tower of London, "with child by the Lord Admiral."

Seymour was beheaded soon afterwards, but the most tragic of all the Tudor residents was Jane Grey, daughter of the Duke of Suffolk and great-granddaughter of King Henry VII. At the age of nine, she came to live here for a time with Queen Catherine. Cruelly treated by her parents, she got more kindness from her tutor and responded by becoming an excellent student. By the age of thirteen she was known in England and abroad for her ability to speak as well as write Classical Greek. A visitor to her family home in Leicestershire found her reading Plato while the rest of her family was out hunting.

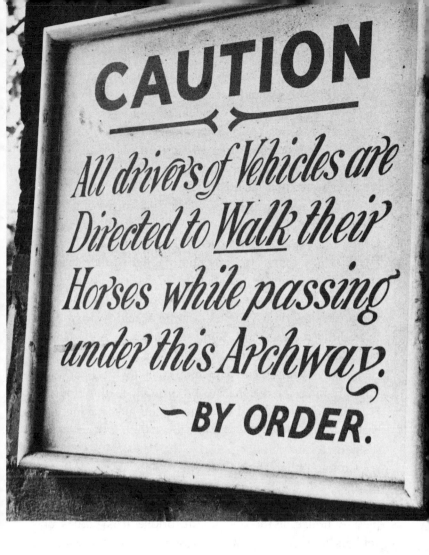

At fifteen she was forced to make a political marriage with Guildford Dudley, son of the powerful Duke of Northumberland. She had at first refused to marry him, but her father beat her into submission. When Henry VIII's son Edward VI died in 1553, Jane was put forward as Queen by her scheming relatives, and she "reigned" for nine days before being overcome by the forces of Henry's daughter, Mary. Under sentence of death, at the age of sixteen, Jane was calm and impressive. From a window in the Tower of London she watched her husband taken off in procession, and a few minutes later saw his headless corpse brought back. Later the same day she went to the scaffold herself. Blindfolded, she was left to grope helplessly for the block, asking "Where is it? What should I do?" A tall executioner dressed in scarlet took off her head. Back in Leicestershire the family servants are said to have cut off the tops of the oak trees as a memorial to their talented and brave Queen Jane.

Come back into Cheyne Walk and turn right. Just ahead is the noisy junction of Chelsea Embankment and Oakley Street. As you approach it, look at **no. 27** Cheyne Walk, on the right. This was Bram Stoker's home in the early 1880s, until he was persuaded to leave it by his wife, who had had a frightening experience here. Stoker, while traveling on a Thames steamboat, had seen an old man climb the rails and drop into the river. Although a rapid and dangerous tide was running, Stoker went in, caught him, and swam with him back to the boat. He then arranged for the man to be brought to this house. He was, however, found to be dead, and after having the corpse in her dining room Mrs. Stoker took a permanent disliking to the place.

Crossing the Thames at this point is the **Albert Bridge**, built in 1873, a masterpiece of ornate Victorian ironwork, using both cantilever and suspension principles. A notice at the end of the bridge tells parties of soldiers to break step while crossing. (Even a massive and soundly built bridge can be brought down by the vibrations of a group of people marching in step.)

Cross Oakley Street to where Cheyne Walk continues, close to a piece of modern sculpture showing a boy and dolphin. Farther along, at **no. 48** Cheyne Walk, the stems of creeping plants twist around the metal supports of a balcony. In the early 1970s this was Mick Jagger's house. Just beyond is the junction of Cheyne Walk and Cheyne Row. The pub on the far corner, The **King's Head and Eight Bells**, is fashionable and very good for lunches. Notice the modern copper-framed gaslights outside. Turn into **Cheyne Row**; 50 yards along on the right is a plaque from the time its oldest houses were built; it's set into the side wall of **no. 16,** about 20 feet up, and reads "This is Cheyne Row, 1708." Above the front door of **no. 18,** and best seen from across the street, is a delicately painted fire mark with the policy number of some long-dead insurer. At **no. 24** (formerly no. 5) is the house of Thomas Carlyle, a biographer and historian revered in his time but now largely forgotten. Carlyle lived here—in what was already an old house—from 1834 until his death in 1881. The house is kept as a museum, as we shall see in a moment. In his work, Carlyle claimed that nations ought to submit to the rule of gifted and heroic leaders, an idea with dangers that are obvious nowadays. (His special admiration for Frederick the Great of Prussia was shared, many years later, by Hitler.) But in private life Carlyle could be extraordinarily generous. As a young writer, he gave much of his small and insecure income to help in his brother's education. And when the philosopher John Stuart Mill lost the only copy of a work that had taken Carlyle months to produce, the author's main concern was to prevent Mill from finding out how much damage he had done.

The house is open from April to October, and a guided tour is given for a small fee. When you ring for admission, you will hear the eighteenth-century bell sounding inside. The interior is almost exactly as it was in Carlyle's day. His hat still hangs in the hall, though now it is discreetly secured to its peg to foil souvenir hunters. On the walls there is full-length wooden paneling: Carlyle was very excited about this, his wife less so. She thought of the bugs that might be living securely behind it.

In the front basement is a fine kitchen with a stone floor. For many years water was pumped from a well below. The kitchen range is a delight of economy; the open fireplace could be regulated to fit different size fires by the movement of one side, and the fire itself heated both a water tank and an oven. Carlyle's woman servant slept in the kitchen; in common Victorian style, she wasn't allowed her own bedroom. Upstairs you will see the four-poster that Mrs. Carlyle brought here (she herself had been born in it). On a windowpane there's a clearly legible bit of graffiti, scratched by a young window cleaner in the 1790s.

Go a few steps farther up Cheyne Row to the first crossroad, **Upper Cheyne Row**, which runs to the left and right. This meeting place of eighteenth-century streets is one of the quietest corners in Chelsea. The narrow entrance to Upper Cheyne Row on the left was designed to let through a single horse-drawn carriage. The iron posts standing near the edge of the sidewalk were to prevent carriages from cutting corners (literally) and endangering pedestrians. Several of the small Georgian houses have pleasant and distinctive lights above their doors; look at nos. 30, 24, and 22.

Turn for a moment into the section of Upper Cheyne Row on the right. The fifth house along, **no. 22**, was in the 1830s the home of Leigh Hunt, a radical journalist and friend of the poets Shelley, Byron, and Keats. Hunt had become famous in 1812 when he clashed with the Prince Regent (later King George IV). A conservative newspaper had stated that the Prince was an "Adonis of loveliness, attended by pleasure, honour, virtue and truth." The reality, however, was rather different. Leigh Hunt and his brother, carried away by love of truth, printed a reply in their own newspaper:

> This Adonis in Loveliness was a corpulent man of fifty. . . . This delightful, blissful, wise, honourable, virtuous, true and immortal prince was a violator of his word, a libertine over head and ears in disgrace, a despiser of domestic ties; the companion of gamblers and demireps [demimondaines], a man who has just closed half a century without one single claim on the gratitude of his country . . .

For this the brothers were sentenced to two years' imprisonment and ordered to pay large fines—unless they promised not to attack the Prince again. They refused, and made themselves minor heroes by going to prison instead. Georgian prisons, though often appalling and disease-ridden places, were in some ways far more liberal than those of today. To make his own cell bearable, Leigh Hunt had roses painted on the walls and a sky scene on the ceiling. He was allowed books and a piano. His wife and famous writers paid him visits.

A few years later, in 1820, Hunt had the satisfaction of seeing his words justified and his royal enemy truly "over head and ears in disgrace." By now George was king and his estranged second wife, Caroline of Brunswick, was in name the Queen of England. In 1820 he tried to divorce her, almost causing a revolution. Troops mutinied, loyalist politicians were mobbed, and large groups of demure and respected citizens demonstrated in support of Caroline. Before the House of Lords, George's representatives tried to prove that the Queen had had an affair with a handsome Italian gentleman named Bergami. She almost certainly had, but the King himself was famous for his mistresses, and the royal accusation of adultery seemed hopelessly hypocritical. One Italian witness, summoned to help the King's case, lost his nerve when confronted with the pomp of the House of Lords and replied in answer to over fifty questions, *"non mi ricordo"* ("I don't remember"). Caroline's supporters were triumphant, and banners waved in London with *"non mi ricordo"* gleefully inscribed. (If you visit the National Portrait Gallery, near Trafalgar Square, look for the large painting of Caroline's "trial" before the Lords. Beside it is displayed a yellowing contemporary copy of a *"non mi ricordo"* poem.) George's case eventually collapsed, perhaps because Caroline's lawyer threatened to reveal that the King was a bigamist. Caroline died in 1821, a few days after being physically shut out of George's Coronation at Westminister Abbey.

By the 1830s Leigh Hunt had fallen on hard times.

While living here he was often unable to buy bread. Carlyle, who had known severe poverty himself, wrote rather callously of the squalor in Hunt's home:

> Hunt's house excels all you have ever read of—a pocket tinkerdom, without parallel even in literature. In his family room, where are a sickly large wife and a whole school of well-conditioned wild children, you will find half-a-dozen old rickety chairs gathered from half-a-dozen different hucksters. . . . On these and around them and over the dusty table and carpet lie all kinds of litter—books, papers, egg-shells, scissors, and last night, when I was there, the torn heart of a loaf. . . .

Like other bold people of the Georgian era, Hunt mellowed with the coming of the Victorian age. He escaped poverty in 1840 by writing a successful romantic play.

Go back to the crossroads, and go through the narrow carriageway straight ahead of you. A few yards farther on, where this road opens into **Lawrence Street,** is a fine row of tiny cottages on the left. On one of them, **no. 19,** is a portrait of Queen Anne, in whose reign they were built. (She was the last Stuart monarch and died in 1714.) Across the road, **no. 15** Lawrence Street is the site of a mid-eighteenth-century pottery, where expensive figures were made in the pastoral style fashionable in France before the revolution. China shepherdesses toyed with pet lambs, and were courted by elegant, leisured shepherds. The factory has now entirely disappeared; its site was rediscovered only in 1970, when innumerable china fragments were unearthed in the garden of no. 15. Several products of the factory have survived and are now highly valued. Thea Holme, in her interesting book on Chelsea, tells of the owner of one china piece who decided in 1929 to auction it, hoping to raise £100 to buy a used car. Instead the object fetched £3,250, enough at the time to buy several houses.

When you are a little farther along Lawrence Street,

turn right for a moment into the narrow **Justice Walk** to look at the magnificently carved doorcase of **no. 6**, 20 yards down on the right. Then come back to Lawrence Street, turn right, and at **no. 11** you will see the tall and elegant bow window of an artist's studio, supported by carved brackets. It's best viewed from across the street, from where you will also see the miniature oval window above it.

A few steps farther down Lawrence Street is a pub, the **Cross Keys.** Inside there is much pleasant old woodwork and in winter an open fire. Good pub lunches are served and also Real Ale (ask for Director's). Tucked away in this quiet street, the place isn't often found by passersby. Instead, it is sought out by knowing customers, who sometimes come from quite a distance and can be quite possessive about "their" pub.

Just beyond the pub, Lawrence Street joins Cheyne Walk. The apartment block on the left corner here, **Carlyle Mansions,** is where the novelist Henry James died in 1916. Turn right into Cheyne Walk, and straight ahead you will see **Chelsea Old Church.** Most of this small building was bombed to bits in 1941 by a land mine probably meant for one of the large power stations nearby. Luckily, the section where least damage was done was the one built in Henry VIII's time by Thomas More.

As you reach the church, you can see an ornate tomb with an urn beneath a canopy of stone. This is the burial place of Hans Sloane, physician and local landlord. Around the urn are carved snakes, symbols of Asclepius, the Greek god of healing. More's chapel is in the corner of the church just behind this tomb. Go along to the left of the church, passing an unfortunate modern statue of More. More is shown dressed almost entirely in somber black but with a golden face; the bulky statue sits looking out towards the river and resembles an elephantine version of a cheap icon.

Go to the end of the church wall, turn right, and you will find the entrance to the church. If you go in, look for the dark slab set into the wall just to the right of the main altar. This is More's epitaph, in Latin and drafted

by More himself some time before his support of the papacy against Henry VIII brought him to the block. The first two words of line one are his name in Latin, *"Thomas Morus."* Now look fifteen lines down where, near the beginning of the line, there's a famous gap. The text reads, *"furibus autem et homicidis*—[blank] *molestus,"* meaning that More was "to thieves, however, and murderers— [blank] an oppressor." Where the blank now stands, More originally intended to write *"et hereticis,"* claiming that he was a persecutor also of heretics. According to the story, he was dissuaded from this boast by the kindly Dutch scholar Erasmus. Although impressive in several ways, More was not quite the gentle, lovable figure portrayed in the film *A Man for All Seasons.* He approved warmly of the execution of humble people for holding unorthodox religious views. Above the stone arch over More's epitaph is the dark face of a Moor, an African. Heraldic devices often involved a pun on the owner's name.

Turn left as you walk away from the altar and go into the little chapel that More built. Here on the wall a brass plate from the 1550s records the burial of Jane Guildford. By the time she died, her husband (the Duke of Northumberland), her son and her daughter-in-law (Jane Grey) had all been executed. A few inches to the right of her epitaph a superb, multicolored brass plate shows a Tudor lady at prayer.

A little farther along the same side of the church are the large alabaster effigies of two grandly named Elizabethan aristocrats, Lord and Lady Dacre of the South. Their effigies lie side by side: she wears the ruff fashionable at the time, and he wears armor. His helmet, not an alabaster copy but the original, hangs above the tomb, a little to the right. Notice, too, that beside his effigy is an alabaster model of a dead infant daughter.

To end this walk, you may like to go along the pleasant **Old Church Street**—the road leading to the right as you leave the church door. In a few hundred yards this will bring you to one of the liveliest parts of the King's Road.

Walk · 5

The Backstairs of Government

WESTMINSTER

AND WHITEHALL

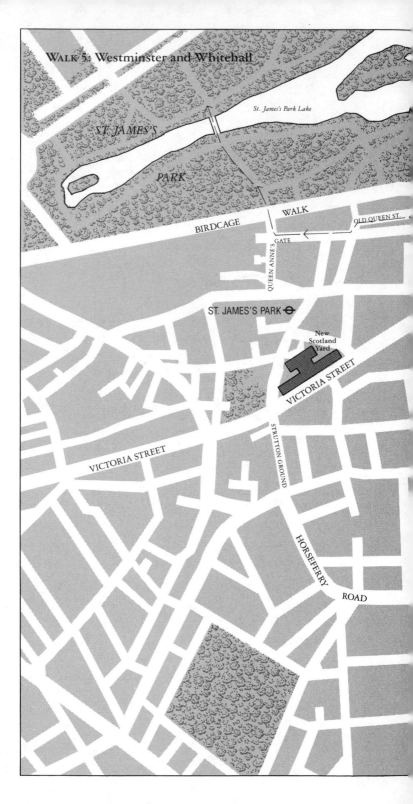

WALK 5: Westminster and Whitehall

ST JAMES'S

St. James's Park Lake

PARK

BIRDCAGE   WALK   OLD QUEEN ST.

QUEEN ANNE'S   GATE

ST. JAMES'S PARK ⊖

New Scotland Yard

VICTORIA STREET

VICTORIA STREET   STRUTTON GROUND

HORSEFERRY   ROAD

The County Hall

WESTMINSTER

GREAT GEORGE STREET

PARLIAMENT

BRIDGE ST.

WESTMINSTER BRIDGE

NEW PALACE YARD

Big Ben

SQUARE

ST. MARGARET ST.

Houses of Parliament

St. Margaret's Church

Westminster Hall

STOREY'S GATE

Westminster Abbey

POETS' CORNER

OLD PALACE YARD

GREAT SMITH ST.

DEAN'S

YARD

Thames

BARTON ST.

Westminster School

GREAT COLLEGE ST.

ABINGDON ST.

VICTORIA TOWER GARDENS

GREAT PETER STREET

MARSHAM STREET

River

MILLBANK

LAMBETH PALACE ROAD

Lambeth Palace

HORSEFERRY ROAD

LAMBETH BRIDGE

MARSHAM STREET

MILLBANK

Starting Point: Westminster tube station
Buses: 3, 11, 12, 24, 29, 53, 77, 77A, 88, 109, 159, 170, 184, C1

On this walk we break one of the rules of our book—by including an obvious place for visitors, the Houses of Parliament. But I hope you would guess by now that our view of Parliament will be unconventional: more comic, and sometimes more somber, than in nervously patriotic guidebooks. After leaving the Parliament buildings, the walk turns away into quiet and handsome back streets of eighteenth-century houses. Today this set of streets contains few residents; property is too expensive for domestic use. And tourists are drawn away by Westminster Abbey, which we won't be visiting. So you'll see hardly any shops or pubs. Instead you'll have almost to yourself one of the most fashionable areas of London two centuries ago.

On emerging from Westminster tube station, you are immediately met—or rather towered over—by Big Ben. The name is applied pedantically to the bell of the clock, but in normal English it means the clock or the whole tower. The "Ben" may come from the name of Benjamin Hall, an official in charge of the bell when it was new, in the 1850s. Turn right from the exit of the tube. After some 100 yards, turn left, and cross at the traffic lights to walk along the whole façade of the **Parliament Buildings.** At first you will have iron railings on your left; 30 yards along, look through the gateway in the railings. This is the scene of one of the most macabre incidents in the recent history of Westminster.

Through the gateway, and slightly to the left, you will see a ramp disappearing underground. It leads to the car park of the House of Commons. On March 30, 1979, a Conservative M.P. and spokesman on Northern Irish affairs, Airey Neave, began driving up this ramp. M.P.s in the House of Commons then heard a large explosion. Since the proceedings of the House were being recorded, television and radio were subsequently able to broadcast round the world the blast which killed Airey Neave. At the time of this writing, no one has been charged with the killing. But it is accepted that it was the work of Irish republicans, who used as detonator a device involving mercury. The mercury was meant to tilt and complete the circuit for explosion when the car was driven on an incline.

Neave was not a prominent M.P., but his importance was great. He led the successful campaign by right-wing Conservatives to replace Edward Heath as party leader with Margaret Thatcher. Thatcher is said to have felt the loss of Neave bitterly. This event probably contributed to the fortitude with which she contemplated the deaths of IRA men on hunger strikes in the early 1980s.

The killing of Neave followed a pattern of Irish warfare which is millennia rather than centuries old and which is still scarcely understood outside Ireland. From Roman times, Celtic warfare has been nongenocidal. Usually it aimed to kill the enemy chief. Celtic society itself centered on chiefs; if the chief was killed, morale and aggression failed. In most of Celtic Europe, the old way of fighting died out as the result of conquest by the Romans and others. But the Romans never invaded Ireland,

and the English conquest had only a superficial impact on most of Irish culture before the nineteenth century.

Celtic techniques of warfare reemerged in the Irish civil war of 1922–23. The losing side, the IRA, showed great reluctance to massacre their Free State opponents; orders were frequently given to fire over their heads. But the IRA did kill the Free State leader, Michael Collins. And Collins himself had arranged the assassination of the leading British soldier in Ireland, General Sir Henry Wilson. Irish republicans often assume that the English will resemble themselves in being smitten when a chief is killed. But the English leaders, who (unlike the Irish) would forgive a massacre of ordinary soldiers, or even of civilians, see the killing of a leader such as Neave or Mountbatten as an act of wickedness rather than an act of war and close ranks accordingly. In neither Ireland nor England is there any tradition of understanding the other country's history.

Leave the gates, and continue along the side of the Parliament buildings. To your left is a low wall. Beyond that is a small lawn with a fairly modern statue of Oliver Cromwell, who led the parliamentary army against Charles I after the latter had tried to degrade Parliament. The long building with the slate roof, behind the statue, is architecturally a key to the whole site. It is **Westminster Hall,** built and remodeled between the eleventh and fourteenth centuries. Most of the buildings of Parliament—the Houses of Commons and Lords, Big Ben, and the rest—are far less old. They were built between 1840 and 1888. But their Gothic architecture was designed to harmonize with the medieval style of Westminster Hall here.

The hall has been used for some of the most emotional of state occasions. At the Coronation of George IV in 1821, a feast for grandees was given here. The lords sat at tables on the floor of the hall and were sumptuously fed. Their wives and families were allowed to watch from galleries above. But the food was not for them. One peer had pity on his family, took a chicken from his table, thoughtfully wrapped it, then hurled it up to the gallery for them to catch.

It was in Westminster Hall that King Charles was tried in 1649, after losing the Civil War—the choice of venue was symbolic of Parliament's victory. Charles refused to recognize the proceedings, saying that he had been appointed King by God and inquiring what higher authority had appointed the court. His two chief opponents, Cromwell and Thomas Fairfax, were later to die peacefully. But in 1660, when Charles's son was allowed back from exile to become Charles II, vengeance on the "regicides" was ferocious. Some of Cromwell's surviving supporters were hanged, drawn, and quartered. Cromwell himself, already dead some two years, might have seemed beyond reprisals. But enthusiastic royalists dug up his corpse from Westminster Abbey and hanged it. Then the head was cut off and displayed for over twenty years from the roof of Westminster Hall—the symbolic site again. In an age when many were illiterate and all were hungry for images, the rotting heads of opponents, displayed at significant places, made wonderful propaganda.

Walk until you are level with Cromwell's statue, then stop for a moment. Across the busy road to your right are the backs of two grand buildings. The smaller of the pair, to the right, is **St. Margaret's Church**, regarded as the parish church of the House of Commons. At a service here in May 1667, Samuel Pepys put his naval telescope ("perspective glass") to a nonmilitary use: as he recounted, he looked, "with my perspective glass, up and down the church, by which I had the pleasure of seeing and gazing at a great many very fine women. And what with that and sleeping I passed away the time till sermon was done." At the time this was a politically correct thing to do. In matters of religion, enthusiasts were likely to be Puritans—the enemies of the King. But in matters of philandering, the King led the pack. The larger building, to the left of St. Margaret's as you look, is **Westminster Abbey**; this eastern end was built in the early 1500s on the orders of Henry VII. Although grimy at the time of writing, its intricate Gothic stonework makes this one of the most impressive parts of the great hybrid building.

Walk 40 yards beyond Cromwell's statue, and you will be level with the entrance to the **House of Commons.** For ourselves, the public, entry here has become difficult in recent years, a result of worries about security and memories of a demonstration in which protesters bespattered M.P.s by throwing down from the public gallery bags of manure, as it was delicately termed in the press. For a casual visit, you may find it possible to get in without waiting in line on a weekday evening (Monday to Thursday), from 9:00 P.M. onward. But to attend one of the great gladiatorial sessions, Prime Minister's Questions on the afternoons of Tuesdays and Thursdays, the best bet is to apply in advance for a ticket from the American embassy.

In a few minutes, when you reach a more pleasant place to stand and view the Houses of Parliament, there'll be some informal detail of what happens behind this august Victorian façade. But first, for a brief detour, walk to the far end of the Parliament buildings, marked by the huge Victoria Tower, about 150 yards ahead of you. Where Parliament ends, a park begins; turn left into the park at the first entry, by the statue of Mrs. Emmeline Pankhurst, the woman suffrage leader, who was actually imprisoned for a short time in Parliament as the result of a demonstration. The path which passes her statue will bring you to the river. On the way you will pass a sculpture by Auguste Rodin, *The Burghers of Calais.* The figures are shown roped and bearing the key to their town. The story is that these leading citizens gave themselves as hostages to Edward III during an English assault on their French coastal town in 1347, and survived.

From Rodin's sculpture, follow the path to the wall which overlooks the Thames. Across the river, slightly to the right as you look, is the medieval **Lambeth Palace**— just this side of Lambeth Bridge. The palace is the official residence of the Primate of the Anglican Church, the

Archbishop of Canterbury. Also across the river, this time to the left and just beyond Westminster Bridge, is a twentieth-century building with green copper casings on its upper windows. This is, or rather was, **County Hall,** the seat until the mid-1980s of the Greater London Council, London's supreme local government body. In its last years as County Hall, this building was the scene of a splendidly public controversy.

The last administration in County Hall was a Labour one, which used much left-wing rhetoric. Its chief, Ken Livingstone, was called "Red Ken" by most of the tabloid press, which duly exploited the financial aid given by his council to certain gay groups. Politicians cast as villainous reds by the British press usually become hysterical and ineffective under the strain. Livingstone alone survived, by remaining endlessly patient in public, however provoked. (I remember one interviewer asking him slyly, "Is it true that you are very close to your mother?")

Livingstone's County Hall in the early 1980s became a showpiece. What it showed was the unemployment figures for London, which were high. Livingstone blamed them on Mrs. Thatcher's government, so the figures were written up on huge billboards and mounted on the roof of the building, to confront the Prime Minister and her supporters across the river. For such public insubordination, Thatcher abolished the Greater London Council. Livingstone then published a book, titled with the anarchist slogan *If Voting Changed Anything, They'd Abolish It,* patiently submitted himself to another vote, was elected M.P., and crossed the river to sit in Parliament.

Retrace the route past Mrs. Pankhurst's statue to the main road; cross it, turn right, cross Great College Street and stand on the lawn beside the sculpture by Henry Moore. (Officially the work is entitled *Knife Edge Two Piece.*) At the edge of the lawn, level with the Victoria Tower, is a medieval structure, the **Jewel Tower,** where

Jewel Tower

Edward III reportedly kept his valuables. It is all that remains of the domestic palace of Westminster, where Kings lived, which became the seat of Parliament because it was where royal advisers gathered. The term *Palace of Westminster* lives on, but now only as a name for the Parliament buildings.

From this lawn you get one of the finest views of the Houses of Parliament. This may be the place for a few details and stories from Parliament's recent history. The tower overlooking the park, the **Victoria Tower,** has at its base the gate where the sovereign's carriage enters for the ceremonial opening session of Parliament every autumn. The sovereign then goes into the House of Lords. From here you can also see the peers' own entrance to the **House of Lords:** this is marked by the stone canopy some 70 yards from the Victoria Tower.

Since the nineteenth century, the House of Lords has been a backwater; it now has occasional value through adding to, or delaying, legislation which originates in the Commons. Most peers are hereditary, and most are Conservatives. This oddity is tolerated for two main reasons: The Lords cannot on their own make or unmake legislation, and most members of the Lords rarely or never turn up. In a crisis, the Conservatives import backwoods peers to win a vote. For a rare ceremony, such as the Queen's Jubilee assembly in Westminster Hall, there converges a host of backwoods men. During the Jubilee, in 1977, rumors reached the press that some peers were turning up for the ceremony, signing in for their attendance money (peers are paid only for each day they attend), and then asking officials how they could find the House of Lords.

Normal attendance on the red-leather benches of the Lords is wretchedly thin. Debates seem to lack all adrenaline; it is as if speakers sense that they are talking into a void. Aging politicians from the Commons are sometimes "promoted" to the Lords. This is known in parliamentary slang as being "kicked upstairs." Most members of the Commons are quite happy about the obvious weakness of the Lords. To improve the Lords would increase the influence of the Upper House, and that would reduce the power of the Commons.

The House of Commons is a place of greater uproar, and of more obvious aggression, than the United States Congress. With my British background, I was pleasantly amazed, on my first visit to Congress in Washington, to see politicians' spouses and children strolling around the chamber during a business session. That, of course, helps to produce an easy atmosphere. But in the British House of Commons there is no such relaxation. The green-leather benches are arranged in adversarial rows; Opposition members confront the Government. In front of the two opposing blocks of benches are lines marked on the floor; these derive from the time when rival members had to be restrained from sword-fighting. Speakers are forbidden to go beyond their lines, and the distance between the two lines is more than two swords' length. But colorful disorder still goes on. In the 1970s a leading Conservative, Michael Heseltine—along with many of his colleagues—believed that the Labour Government had cheated to win a close vote in the Commons. Angrily he picked up the ceremonial mace, symbol of the Speaker's authority, and brandished it at the Labour benches. At that point, in the words of the BBC's parliamentary reporter, "Fighting broke out all over the House."

The general atmosphere of the Commons is often described as masculine and clubbish. Members express their rivalry—and underlying solidarity—by taking part in football matches, Labour against Conservative. The masculine spirit helps to explain the traditionally low number of women M.P.s. Of those women who do enter—and survive—the House, many are honorary men. Mrs. Thatcher, in her early days as Prime Minister, was observed by a journalist doodling on her Order Paper in the Commons. The subject of her doodle, the journalist reported, was a large dagger.

To deal with the risk of excessive uproar in the Commons, rules of "parliamentary language" have evolved. Emotive words must be avoided. It is forbidden, for example, to say that members of the rival party are "asleep" in the chamber. Instead they must be described as "resting with their eyes closed." "That's a lie" is also forbidden. The required phrase, deliberately cumbersome, is "terminological inexactitude." More ingeniously, parliamentarians have realized that one of the most emotive and confrontational of words is *you.* So "you" is forbidden and replaced by "The Honourable Member," "The Honourable Lady," and the like. "You're a bloody liar" thus becomes "The Honourable Gentleman is a habitual committer of terminological inexactitude."

In the heat of a debate, however, much plain and offensive language is used. The Speaker is then asked to rule on whether the remarks are out of order. Here selective deafness comes into play. The Speaker does not like to reprimand M.P.s, especially the more important ones, so he often claims not to have heard. But when, fairly recently, one M.P. shouted at an opponent "You bastard!" the Speaker did hear. And he was urged by other M.P.s to reprimand their abusive colleague. "Mr. Speaker," they cried, "is that parliamentary language?" The Speaker thought for a moment, then replied, "I understand that in some parts of the country that word is used as a term of affection."

As is usual with the strange doings of otherwise intelligent people, there is some logic behind the noise and fury of the House of Commons. For one thing, most work by M.P.s is done in much calmer conditions, during thinly attended debates which frequently last beyond midnight and in behind-the-scenes committee rooms. The famous rows are usually reserved for the brief twice-weekly sessions of Prime Minister's Questions. The M.P.s need this passion to enliven their sober routine.

But the Commons is also a safety valve for the voters, for whom the British electoral system brings much frus-

tration. Under the British system there is no question of the kind of power-sharing which often happens in the United States, where a President of one party may work alongside a Congress dominated by the other. In Britain a Prime Minister *is* Prime Minister through being able to control a majority of votes in the Commons. So, almost by definition, the Prime Minister and Cabinet dominate the legislature, and there is no written constitution to restrain them. In the 1980s the phrase "elective tyranny," coined by a leading Conservative, was much used. Opposition M.P.s, and the people who elected them, usually look forward to years of powerlessness, without even the prospect of a general election at a fixed time. An election must happen at least every five years, but the Government of the day chooses the exact date to suit its own chances of reelection. (In 1966 a Labour Cabinet discussed whether to time the election to exploit the euphoria expected to result from that year's World Cup Soccer competition.)

Pent-up feelings in the electorate are all the more important because of the way M.P.s are chosen. More than half a dozen parties split the vote in a General Election. The winning party, perhaps gaining a huge majority in the Commons, rarely gets a majority of the popular vote but instead is the party with the largest minority vote. In other words, the majority of voters nearly always get a government they opposed at the polls. A passionate House of Commons helps to calm this powerless majority, by presenting the spectacle of ministers challenged, shouted at and sometimes humiliated.

From close to the Jewel Tower, a high wall borders the lawn and runs to Great College Street. Over the top of the wall from here you can see buildings of Westminster School; there'll be stories to tell about the school when we get closer to it in a few minutes. Walk parallel with the wall, with your back to Parliament, until you reach **Great College Street**; then turn right. Walk to the second street on the left, Barton Street, stopping for a moment before you turn into the street. On the corner where you're now standing, a house of Great College Street has a bracket which once held an eighteenth-century oil lamp. On the opposite corner is one of the last gas lamp standards to be put up; on its base is a plate giving its date as 1910.

Turn into **Barton Street.** Its eighteenth-century houses are prized now for their nearness to Parliament. M.P.s who live here can sit at their firesides of an evening, away from the onerous debates, and need only stroll across the road at the last minute to take part in the required vote when the debating ends.

Look across the road at **no. 14** Barton Street. In 1920–21, this was the home of T. E. Lawrence, "Lawrence of Arabia." In the fourth-story attic he wrote his most famous work, *The Seven Pillars of Wisdom.* In traditional romantic style he described the attic as his "garret"; he reported that for lack of heating he wrote in a flying suit. This urban backwater was a refuge from the storm of publicity he had created for himself, in collaboration with the talented American publicist Lowell Thomas. After the holocaust of the First World War in Europe, and the squalor of the Western Front, public taste was ready for the image of an unsullied hero, who had won a war on a human scale, with white robes amid the clean desert in the land of the Crusaders.

In *The Seven Pillars* Lawrence promoted his image with wildly magnificent boasting—"I wrote my will across the sky in stars"; "Damascus had seemed a sheath for my sword." Then he turned from the legend and from himself in revulsion, changing his surname first to Ross and then to Shaw, and burying himself at the lowest rank first of the air force, then of the army. The range and power of Lawrence's mind are indisputable. He published an acceptable translation of the *Odyssey* from the Greek and the official technical handbook for a naval motor-launch. But for most of the details of the desert campaign against the Turks which made his name there is only one literate source—Lawrence.

Lawrence's civilian life left a trail of anecdotes by third

parties. One story comes from an American archaeologist who visited the prehistoric site at Carchemish on the Euphrates, which Lawrence excavated just before the First World War. She was properly horrified that the coffee Lawrence offered her was served in a Hittite cup, over 3,000 years old. Wasn't he afraid that it would break? Lawrence told her not to worry: "The British Museum will thankfully accept the pieces."

I myself knew two people who claimed firsthand knowledge of Lawrence. One, an old factory clerk in Leicester named Charlie Weston, told me that he had served in the air force with Lawrence. He spoke of the oddity of Lawrence's position; there he was, just an air-craftman, "but we knew he was a colonel in the army." And Lawrence ate in the officer's mess. When I pressed him for more details, Weston gave as a further oddity that Lawrence used to salute when speaking to an officer *on the phone.* It is very unlikely that Weston knew how well this story fits with the pleasure Lawrence is known to have taken in degrading himself. Lawrence's own phrase was "the luxury of taking orders from fools."

My other informant, who was quite close to Lawrence and published a small book about their friendship, was the novelist Henry Williamson, nowadays best remembered for his nature books, notably *Tarka the Otter.* Williamson told me that Lawrence, whose birth was illegitimate, had been emotionally scarred by his mother, a fervent Protestant who inflicted her sense of sexual guilt upon her children. Williamson told me that he believed Lawrence in his unhappiness would have been glad to die when he did, prematurely, as the result of a motorbike crash in 1935.

Now back to the corner of Barton and Great College streets. Turn left, and walk the 50 yards until Great College Street ends. A road now runs to the left, but you should turn to the right, through one of the pair of gateways. Once through the gateway you are in **Dean's Yard.** Walk on the pavement to the right. Here you will see a grand eighteenth-century doorway bearing the number 17. There are torch extinguishers outside, and the fanlight above the door was designed to hold a portable oil lamp. You may see a modern version respectfully in its place. A sense of history is at work here; this is the house of the headmaster of **Westminster School.**

Westminster is what is known in Britain as a Public School. "Public School" means a long-established and expensive private school, with great social cachet. For over two centuries the Public Schools have trained and molded the British ruling class. Most judges, diplomats, top civil servants, senior military officers, and leading financiers are from Public Schools. A recent survey found that two Public Schools, Eton and Winchester, between them supplied fifty—about one in six—Conservative M.P.s.

Almost every British person can produce a lively caricature of a Public School boy. (The phrase includes adult alumni; once a Public School boy, always a Public School boy.) Nicknames for them proliferate. In recent years the louder and less impressive Public School products have been known as Chinless Wonders and Hooray Henries. The female versions are Ra Ra Carolines—from the alleged habit of cheering school hockey teams with shouts of "hurrah." But for most British people a Public School accent is intimidating. A colorful experiment was done recently in London. Each night at a theater the same set of instructions was given to successive audiences, but in a different accent each time. The accent which produced by far the greatest compliance was the Public School one.

The ambivalent attitude toward the Public School product, resentment and respect, is one of the demons of the British psyche. Comedians, most notably the Public School boy John Cleese, get vast applause for their impressions of Hooray Henries. The Monty Python team staged a contest for the Upper Class Twit of the Year. Events included slamming the sports car door after midnight to see who could wake the most neighbors, and seeing who took the longest to undress a debutante after the Hunt Ball. British people would like to believe that Public School boys in general are Upper Class Twits. Sadly, perhaps, part of their psyche is telling them something else. In most structures of British society, ordinary voices fall silent at the sound of a Public School accent.

Westminster School was founded in the Middle Ages; it trained young men for the monastery ("minster") here. When Henry VIII abolished the monastery, in the 1540s, the school survived. In the Civil War a century later, it took the side of King Charles, unlike most of London. But calls to suppress the school were unsuccessful. The list of its famous Old Boys includes Christopher Wren, the dramatist John Dryden, the philosopher John Locke, Edward Gibbon, who wrote *The Decline and Fall of the Roman Empire*, Charles Wesley, and a number of eighteenth-century Prime Ministers. The school had its heyday in the seventeenth and eighteenth centuries. That was the period when Westminster School established the idea in England that aristocrats and gentlemen should send their sons away to board at Public School.

Going away to board meant the traumatic abandonment of family. Only apart from the family could characters be homogenized and loyalties be widened to include a large section of the elite. This weakening of family influence is probably responsible for the enduring power and cohesiveness of the Public School alumni in adult life—the Old Boy Network as it is called in Britain. One little boy, sent to Westminster in 1786, wrote the following letter after his first day and night at the school:

My dear, dear Mother,

If you don't let me come home, I die—I am all over ink, and my fine clothes have been spoilt—I have been tossed in a blanket, and seen a ghost.

I remain, my dear, dear, mother,
Your dutiful and most unhappy son,
Freddy

P.S. Remember me to my father.

Freddy had obviously undergone the initiation rites reserved for the youngest boys. Lacking family affections, some of the boys turned to pets. The future poet William Cowper kept a mouse at Westminster during the 1740s, in the drawer of his desk.

I kept it till it produced six young ones, and my transports [of joy] when I first discovered them cannot easily be conceived, any more than my mortification, when, going to visit my little family, I found that Mouse herself had eaten them! I turned her loose in indignation, and vowed never to keep a mouse again.

Another source of comfort here was snuggling up to other boys. Sharing beds was normal, except for the sons of aristocrats—"quality children," as they were called. It is still a commonplace in Britain that male homosexuality has upper-class overtones. (This is not true of the female kind; traditionally, far fewer girls have gone to boarding school.) With homosexuality at school went secrecy, the adolescent couples or small groups protecting themselves against discovery not only by authority but also by their peers. From this furtive background came several famous spies of the mid-twentieth century. Of these, perhaps the one who gave Stalin the most help by identifying British agents was Kim Philby. After years in British Intelligence he fled to Moscow and became a colonel in the KGB. Philby had been at school (with, he claimed, much eroticism) here at Westminster.

In the eighteenth-century at Westminster School, discipline scarcely existed. The ratio of teachers to pupils was about 1 to 50, and teachers ("masters") could be viewed with some disdain as belonging to a lower social class than the boys. One teacher had his hair set on fire by young Lord March, who was then obliged to beat the teacher's head in order to put out the blaze. The teachers knew that their small authority had to be used sparingly, and strategically, in cases where it might work. As the adult Cowper put it, addressing the teachers of Westminster in verse:

> But ye connive at what ye cannot cure,
> And evils, not to be endured, endure
> Lest power exerted, but without success,
> Should make the little ye retain still less.

Cowper's poem about the school, *Tirocinium*, suggests that the older schoolboys were involved in theft and gambling, drinking and occasional whoring. Reform of the Public Schools came in the mid-nineteenth century. Since then, such schools have flourished most at safe distances from the vice of large towns. The pattern remains to this day, so for over a century Westminster has suffered from its inner-city position. It is no longer seen as a social rival to Eton. But academic standards are high. In the 1960s, when the Labour Prime Minister Harold Wilson was abolishing the national system of genuinely public academic schools (grammar schools) as being elitist and divisive, he sent his own son to Westminster.

Continue along the pavement. A few yards beyond the headmaster's house, the first entry on the right is worth discreet exploration—and not just to read the sign in many languages telling you to go no farther. From here is the best view of the Westminster School buildings. Then return to Dean's Yard, turn right and head for the gateway diagonally opposite the one which brought you in. On the way, notice the delicate stems of early-nineteenth-century gas lamps.

On emerging from the archway, you will see to your right the entry to Westminster Abbey. However, turn left and go to the traffic lights a few yards away. Cross the main road (Victoria Street) at the lights; then walk into the street **(Storey's Gate)** which virtually continues the line you took while crossing the main road. Walk along the left of Storey's Gate, and turn into the second entry on the left—**Old Queen Street**. After about 100 yards, Old Queen Street bends slightly to the left and becomes **Queen Anne's Gate**—a showpiece since the time of its construction, 1704.

The tall, flat-fronted buildings of Queen Anne's Gate were designed to hold large retinues of servants, as well as the aristocrats who employed them. And the roadway outside was made wide enough to give turning space to the grandest of transport, the six-horse carriage. The conical link extinguishers outside some of the doors recall the nights two centuries ago when torches blazed to escort the great. And above many doors are elaborately carved wooden canopies. A statue of Queen Anne, made in her lifetime when the street was new, stands across the road, by no. 15. It is worth a close look as a record of early-eighteenth-century dress. (Anne herself had the desperate misfortune to give birth to fourteen children who, through some genetic disorder, all died young. She

was alleged to have sought relief in the bottle and was nicknamed "Brandy Nan.")

No. 20, on the right, was the birthplace—in 1784—of a future Prime Minister, Lord Palmerston. It is said that nostalgic civil servants in Britain still sigh for the days of Palmerston, the Days When Britain Mattered. In cases where an American President today might send in the bombers, or the marines, Palmerston sent a gunboat. Or so he is remembered. Palmerston took the lead in founding the state of Belgium, removing the Turks from much of Greece and annexing Hong Kong. He refrained (just) from allying Britain with the Confederate States in the American Civil War. But perhaps the best stories to tell in Queen Anne's Gate are of two people who knew the place well in its eighteenth-century heyday, although their former houses, a few yards away, cannot now be traced. First, there is the grim figure of the politician Lord North, then a gloriously successful Irish actress, Peg Woffington.

Lord North is rightly remembered as George III's chief agent in bringing on war with the American colonies. The fatal British decision to persist with the tax on tea was taken by the Cabinet in 1770; it was North who proposed it, and his motion was passed by a majority of one. North reveled in his oligarchic values; he boasted that in many years he had not once voted for a popular measure. (For aristocrats like North, *popular* and *democratic* were emotive words.) He passionately defended the traditional refusal to publish the debates of Parliament; if the common people knew what their masters were saying, untold mischief would ensue. Instead, illicit transcripts were published by radicals under thin disguises: "Proceedings of the Robin Hood Club, meeting at Westminster." (North's spirit is not wholly dead; only in 1989 did the House of Commons relax its ban on the televising of debates, against prime ministerial advice.)

North and King George were for long very close. They were even similar in appearance; the King's father is supposed to have joked to North's father that one of their

Panels from Georgian water tanks, Queen Anne's Gate

wives must have been cheating. Late in his life North
went blind; King George went mad. In an interval of san-
ity, George suggested that the parallel afflictions of the
two men were God's punishment for fighting (or losing?)
the American war. During his career as chief minister,
North's dislike of the masses was cordially returned.
However, he benefited from the relative gentleness which
had come over British political life after the seventeenth-
century Civil War. In Britain, even the riots were re-

strained. Rioters who surrounded and besieged Lord North contented themselves with destroying his carriage and victoriously carrying off his hat. In France at the time, radicals were demanding something more solid.

This neighborhood was also the home of Peg Woffington, a sensational actress of the mid-eighteenth century. It's pretty unpromising to try to evoke in print the skills of actors (or musicians), but we can make out a sympathetic picture of Woffington's turbulent life. Her mother was the impoverished widow of an Irish bricklayer, who made a living by selling fruit and watercress in Dublin. The mother also hired out her baby daughter, Peg. She, along with another baby, was put into a basket and secured to the leg of a tightrope walker. The acrobat's feat was to balance at a dangerous height without spilling either of the babies. As a young adult, Woffington had success on the stage in Dublin and then came to London, where she made a fortune for her financial backers. She was described as a "bold-faced Irish girl" and "the handsomest woman who ever appeared on the stage."

The stage, then as now, was a platform for social advancement. Many of the finest actresses, like Nell Gwynne, quickly disappeared into aristocratic beds. Lavinia Fenton, who triumphantly played Polly Peachum at the opening of *The Beggar's Opera*, vanished shortly afterwards, to reemerge in even greater triumph as the Duchess of Bolton, with a large private income from His Grace the Duke. This process deprived the public of many of their favorite performers. But Peg Woffington did not succumb. We can imagine the sort of offers she must have had from the fact that her sister, mainly on the strength of Peg's reflected glory, married the son of an earl.

Although the young man was far from rich, such a marriage could not normally have been expected by the daughter of a provincial watercress seller. The story goes that at first the Earl was appalled at the thought of his son married to the sister of an actress. Actresses, after all, were loose women. But, on meeting the stylish Peg,

he is said to have condescended; the marriage might be tolerated. Peg Woffington, however, was not to be patronized. For one thing, it was her money which kept her sister and now was keeping the sister's husband. She told the Earl, "My Lord, I have much more reason to be offended at the marriage than Your Lordship, for whereas I had before but one beggar to support, I now have two."

Woffington's most famous liaison was with the actor-manager David Garrick. For a time she lived in a threesome with Garrick and another man. As a Victorian author was later to note dryly, "This unpromising experiment speedily broke down." There were many other affairs. A common virtuoso feat for beautiful actresses in the eighteenth century was to play male roles. On one occasion, after Woffington had done so, she supposedly said to a male colleague, "I have played the part so oft that half the town believe me to be a real man." To which the man replied, "Madam, the other half *know* you to be a woman."

Woffington was noted for her consideration toward audiences, playing even when ill. She also provided generously for the support of her elderly mother. But she was not a lay saint. Contemporary men were stimulated by the thought of attractive actresses as vicious rivals of each other, and egged the women on. Gleeful reports circulated about the brawl Woffington had with another Irish star of the English stage, Kitty Clive, and about her backstage row with rival actress George Anne Bellamy. Bellamy, while playing a subordinate part to Woffington's Cleopatra, outshone the Queen of Egypt by appearing in extravagantly beautiful clothes. For this Woffington scolded her behind the scenes; tempers rose, and Woffington suggested that Bellamy had got the expensive clothes as "immoral earnings" from the politician Charles James Fox. Bellamy allegedly replied that she was sorry that "half the town" had been unable to provide similar rewards for Woffington.

In May 1757 Woffington collapsed on stage and thereafter wasted away. She died in her house near here on March 28, 1760.

Walk along Queen Anne's Gate until it forms a **T**-junction. Here you may care to end the walk by turning left: St. James's Park tube station is visible about 100 yards away. But if you turn right, there's a much prettier setting in which to end. After turning right, cross the main road which you will immediately see. It is called **Birdcage Walk,** because Charles II had an aviary for exotic fowl nearby. Then take the path which begins by the traffic lights and leads slightly to the left, into **St. James's Park** proper. This will bring you to a footbridge over an artificial lake, the scene of a very low-key but satisfying London tradition.

At the northern—the far—end of the bridge there stand usually one or two men who have tamed some of the shyest of all birds, house sparrows. They hold out seed, and the birds come to hand. The seed is handed out cheerfully—and free—to visitors, and the sparrows trust them too. This bird behavior interested me, since it is apparently learned and not instinctive. Part of the reason is that in this area there are virtually no resident families, so one important enemy of wildlife—the unsupervised boy—is absent. One of the regular feeders told me that in the spring he sees hen sparrows teaching their young to come to hand. That, seemingly, is how instinct is overcome, or perhaps it is just that sparrows' normal shyness is itself learned by young birds. J. T. Smith, the author of an early guidebook called *The Streets of London*, says about this lakeside, "Even the timid sparrows grow bold, and come to be fed, scores at a time." Smith was writing just before 1850, so we may have here a century and a half of human and bird tradition. You can't help wondering how much further back the tradition may go—perhaps to the late 1600s, when Charles II used to walk by the artificial lake made here for him, "amid crowds of spectators, feeding his ducks."

Look up from the bridge, and before you is one of the best views in London, and a quite un-English one: the Gothic turrets of government buildings in Whitehall, seen across the waters of the lake.

Company, St. James's Park

Restaurants, Pubs, and Shops

Restaurants

COVENT GARDEN

Simeoni's, 43 Drury Lane, WC2, tel. 836-8296. Well-cooked, moderately priced Italian food.

Tutton's, 11 Russell Street, WC2, tel. 836-1167. Cheerful and crowded at midday and evening. Waitresses penetrate the crush with marvelous efficiency. Youngish clientele; food a good value and inexpensive.

Porter's, 17 Henrietta Street, WC2, tel. 836-6466. A creditable imitation of Tutton's, specializing in pies.

Rule's, 35 Maiden Lane, WC2, tel. 836-5314. Fairly expensive and sedate, with fine Victorian furnishings. Traditional English as well as French recipes. Reservations advised.

Fish & Chips, 47 Endell Street, WC2.

ST. JAMES'S

Martinez, 25 Swallow Street, W1, tel. 734-4921. Authentically Spanish, and much frequented by prosperous Spaniards. Immaculate formal service and interesting food. Sherry bar and large 1920s dining room, both decorated with Spanish tiles. Prices moderate.

Wheeler's, 12a Duke of York Street, SW1, tel. 839-7137. Specializes in oysters and flatfish (Dover sole). Very small, intimate rooms. Reservations advised. Prices medium to high.

Colombina, 4–5 Duke of York Street, SW1, tel. 930-8279. Competent, with moderately priced Italian food.

CHELSEA

Topolino D'Ischia, 5 Draycott Avenue, SW3, tel. 584-4003. Informal, good, fairly inexpensive Italian food.

Drake's, 2a Pond Place, SW3, tel. 584-4555. Air-conditioned and therefore by English standards rather posh. Good British cooking.

Victor's, 151 King's Road, SW3, tel. 352-0202. Imaginatively and assertively presented Italian food. Fixed, moderate price. No written menu; you have to ask.

Johnny's Fish Bar, 494 King's Road, SW3. Highly praised fish and chips, to eat on or off the premises.

OFF YOUR ROUTE BUT EXCEPTIONAL VALUE

Natraj, 93 Charlotte Street, W1, tel. 637-0050 (Goodge Street tube station). Nepalese food—a mild, creamy version of Indian.

Pubs

COVENT GARDEN

Lamb & Flag, 33 Rose Street, WC2. Ancient, dignified building and furnishings. Strong beer and good food, including a selection of cheeses and pâtés. For lunch, try to arrive before 12:30; the place soon fills with Covent Garden's media people.

Marquis of Anglesey, 39 Bow Street, WC2. Unpretentious and pleasant. A narrow choice of food, but fair value. The bar on the second story is often a peaceful place to eat.

Nag's Head, 10 James Street, WC2. Plusher than most Covent Garden pubs, with young, prosperous clientele.

INNS OF COURT

Princess Louise, 208 High Holborn, WC1. Magnificent antique woodwork. A delight for the connoisseur of bitter beer, with many of the fashionable English provincial brews. Men will find impressive stonework and metalwork in a surprising part of the building.

The George, 213 The Strand (corner of Devereux Court). Recommended for its special lunch section, towards the back of the bar.

Cheshire Cheese, 145 Fleet Street, EC4. Expensive and famous tourist trap. W. B. Yeats and friends discussed poetry here.

El Vino's, 47 Fleet Street, EC4. A meeting place for many of London's grander journalists. Women, curiously, are not served at the bar—in spite of legal action by feminists.

Restaurants, Pubs, and Shops

ST. JAMES'S

St. James's has few pubs, but two are good. They are both called **The Red Lion**. One is in Duke of York Street, SW1, with a very small but splendid Victorian interior. The other is in Crown Passage, SW1, and serves good pies at lunchtime.

CHELSEA

Markham Arms, (next to) 138 King's Road, SW3. Once dingy and half-forgotten, until colonized by Mary Quant and her friends. Now brassy and successful, with a fine exterior.

Queen's Elm, 241 Fulham Road (on corner of Old Church Street). Discreetly chic. Some of the wooden furnishings are rickety, others magnificent. Regular patrons very possessive.

King's Head and Eight Bells, 50 Cheyne Walk, SW3. Pleasant interior and famous lunches. Often crowded on weekends.

Cross Keys, Lawrence Street, SW3. More casual, but still with good lunches. Open fire in winter.

Shops

COVENT GARDEN

Naturally British, 13 New Row, WC2, tel. 240-0551. Well-made toys and attractive household goods. Good for presents. Not cheap.

Arthur Middleton, 12 New Row, WC2, tel. 836-7042. Antique scientific instruments.

Neal's Yard (half hidden in the triangle formed by Neal Street, Shorts Gardens and Monmouth Street). A delightful and placid courtyard, with a dovecoat and a dairy that sells sybaritic ice creams and cheeses.

The Kite Store, 69 Neal Street, WC2, tel. 836-1666. The name says it best.

Laura Ashley, 35–36 Bow Street, WC2, tel. 240-1997. Fine furnishings and dress fabrics.

CHELSEA

Chelsea has two antique markets—indoor bazaars with open-front booths. The atmosphere is informal. Bargains are hard to find, but many stalls are a delight to look at. **Antiquarius**, 15 Flood Street (corner of Flood Street and King's Road), SW3, tel. 351-1145. **Chelsea Antique Market**, 245A King's Road, SW3, tel. 352-1425.

Laura Ashley, 157 Fulham Road, SW3, tel. 584-6939. Dresses. Other Laura Ashley shops are at 71 Lower Sloane Street, SW1, tel. 730-1771 (dress fabrics), and 40 Sloane Street, SW1, tel. 235-9728 (wallpaper and fabrics), and in Covent Garden (see above).

Index

Accents, 29, 61–62, 66, 234
Adam, James, 24, 37
Adam, Robert, 24, 37, 40, 42
Adam Street, 37, 40–42
Adam, William, 24, 37
Adelphi, 24, 37–42
Adelphi Terrace, 37–38, 39
Adelphi Theatre, 44
Albert, Prince Consort, 195
Albert Bridge, 206
Albert Victor, Prince, 117–18
Ambassador's Court, 165–66
American Embassy, 13
American Revolution, 148, 240
Anne of Cleves, 204
Anne, Queen, 210, 237–39
Apple Tree Yard, 136–38
Arkwright, Richard, 42
A to Z (maps), 17–18
Australian High Commission, 13

Babington, Anthony, 86
Bacon, Francis, 31

Ballad of Reading Gaol, The
    (Wilde), 190
Bardot, Brigitte, 181
Barristers, 78–79, 91, 95–96,
    98–99, 100–2, 114
Barry, Charles, 87
Barton Street, 230–33
Bateman, H. M., 98
"Bed & breakfast" accommoda-
    tions (b & b's), 7–8
Bedford, Earls (later Dukes) of,
    25, 48, 80
Bedfordbury, 51
Bedford Street, 47–50
Beer, 10–11
Bellingham, John, 82
Bell Yard, 102–4
Berry Bros. and Rudd (wine
    merchants), 155, 156–58,
    159–60
Bertie, Robert, Earl of Lindsey, 81
Big Ben, 219–20
Birdcage Walk, 243

Index

Blackwell, Elizabeth, 195–96
Blake, William, 133, 134
Bleak House (Dickens), 53, 84, 94
Bloomsbury, 7, 84
Blue Ball Yard, 148–49
Boodle's Club, 145–47
British Museum, 7, 71
Brooks's Club, 144, 147–48
Buckingham, George Villiers, Duke of, 29–31
Buckingham Palace, 130
Buckingham Street, 31–37
Bury Street, 142–43
Buses, 5–6
Butler, Samuel, 56

Canadian High Commission, 13
Carey Street, 99–101
Carlton House Terrace, 165
Carlyle, Thomas, 207–8, 210
Carlyle Mansions, 211
Caroline of Brunswick, Queen, 134, 163–64, 209
Carroll, Lewis (Charles Dodgson), 202
Celtic society, 220–21
Central Market, 25, 60, 62–63
Chambers, Sir William, 42
Chapel Market, 9
Chapel Royal, 163, 164, 166–68
Charing Cross Station, 26, 28
Charke, Charlotte, 69–73
Charles I, King, 30, 31, 35, 131, 166, 221, 222, 234
Charles II, King, 35, 69, 80, 81, 89, 93, 114, 116, 131, 153, 155, 162, 166–67, 184, 222, 243
Charlotte, Princess, 134–36, 164
Chelsea, 177–213
  pubs in, 206, 211, 249
  restaurants in, 247
  shops in, 177, 180–81, 250

Chelsea Old Church, 196, 211–13
Cheyne Mews, 202–4
Cheyne Row, 206–8
Cheyne Walk, 178, 196–202, 206, 211–13
Churches, 42–43, 48–50, 60–61, 62, 91–93, 111–13, 131–36, 163, 164, 166–68, 211–13, 222
Cinemas, 11
City Limits (magazine), 11–12
Civil War, American, 195, 239
Civil Wars, British, 31, 166, 222, 234
Clarence House, 165
Clement V, Pope, 124, 125
Cleopatra's Needle, 40
Clover Mews, 193
Cockney speech, 61–62, 66
Collcutt and Hamp (architects), 39, 40
Common Sense (Paine), 81
Communist Party, British, 50
County Hall, 224
Covent Garden, 7, 24, 25–26, 43–73, 80
  gaslights in, 1, 25, 43–44, 60
  ghosts in, 44–45
  Jones's design for, 48, 60
  pubs in, 56–57, 66, 248
  restaurants in, 45–47, 63, 63–65, 246
  shops in, 9, 51, 66–67, 249–50
Cowper, William, 235, 236
Crime and criminals, 4, 10, 25, 32, 38–39, 45, 48–50, 72, 83, 118, 133, 179
Croft, Sir Richard, 134–36
Cromwell, Oliver, 93, 166, 221, 222
Crown Passage, 160

Cruikshank, George, 150–51, 158, 163
Cruikshank, Robert, 150–51
Cumberland, Ernest Augustus, Duke of (later King of Hanover), 142, 158, 169–70
Curious Herbal, A (Blackwell), 195

Daily Express, 12
Daily Mail, 12
Daily Mirror, 12
Daily Telegraph, 12
David Copperfield (Dickens), 32, 37
Dean's Yard, 233
Despard, Edward, 81–82
Devereux (pub), 122
Dickens, Charles, 24, 25–26, 28, 32, 37, 39, 42–43, 45, 53, 54–56, 61, 84–85, 94, 99, 122, 198
Dilke Street, 193
Disraeli, Benjamin, 91
Dodgson, Charles. See Carroll, Lewis
Dorset, Charles Sackville, Earl of, 80–81
Doughty Street, 32
Douglas, Alfred, Lord, 189–90
Douglas, John, Marquess of Queensberry, 190, 191
Down and Out in Paris and London (Orwell), 26
Dracula (Stoker), 185–87
Drake, Sir Francis, 120–21
Driving, 6
Drugstores, 13
Druitt, Dr. Lionel, 117
Druitt, Montague, 117
Drury Lane Theater, 67–73
Dryden, John, 56, 234
Dudley, Guildford, 205

Duke of York's Headquarters, 180
Duke of York Street, 136–38
Dukes Hotel, 150
Dundas, Henry (Hal), 91
Duval, Claude, 48–50

Ede and Ravenscroft (barristers' wigs), 102
Edward II, King, 124, 125
Edward III, King, 223, 226
Edward VI, King, 205
Edward VII, King, 45, 79, 143
Eliot, George (Evans, Mary Ann), 171, 178, 198–200
Elizabeth, Queen Mother, 165
Elizabeth I, Queen, 86, 121, 169, 204
Elizabeth II, Queen, 104
Emergency services, 13
Entertainments, guides to, 11–12
Ernest Augustus, King of Hanover (formerly Duke of Cumberland), 142, 158, 169–70
Eton, 142, 233, 236
Evans, Mary Ann. *See* Eliot, George
Exchange Court, 43–44
Executions, 35, 80, 82, 86, 104, 114–15, 166, 205–6

Fielding, John, 129
Financial Times, 12
Fire marks, 53–54, 69, 99, 200, 207
Fires, 32, 53–56, 57, 66, 67, 106, 115–16, 142–43
Fitzherbert, Maria, 163, 164
Fleet Street, 102–6
Floris (perfumers), 140
Forster, John, 84
Fortnum and Mason's (general store), 140
Fountain Court, 119, 120–22

Index

Fowler, Charles, 62

Fox, Charles James, 60–61, 148, 242

Frederick Augustus, Duke of York, 158, 180

French Revolution, 82, 91

Friary Court, 169–70

Gaslights, 1, 25, 43–44, 60, 99, 110, 148, 150, 155, 160, 163, 206, 231, 237

Gay, John, 83

Gentlemen's clubs, 130–31, 143–48, 160

George, The (pub), 123

George II, King, 57–58, 194

George III, King, 42, 82, 130, 144, 148, 169, 239–40

George IV, King, 24, 134, 151, 158, 163–64, 169, 200, 208–9, 221–22

Getty, Paul, 177, 202

Ghost stories, 44–45

Gibbons, Grinling, 134

Gladstone, William, 91

Glossary of British terms, 15–17

Godwin, E. W., 192, 193

Goldsmith, Oliver, 111–12

Goldsmith Building, 110–13

Goodwin's Court, 51–56

Gordon, Lord George, 117

Great College Street, 230–31, 233

Great Fire of 1666, 32, 106, 115–16

Grey, Jane, 204–6, 213

Guardian, 12

Guildford, Jane, 213

Gull, Sir William, 117

Gwynne, Nell, 69, 81, 241

Hampstead, 44, 84

Handel, George Frideric, 65

Hardwick, Philip, 89

Hardy, Thomas, 39–40, 201

Hare Court, 114

"Head Gardener's Castle," 90

Help, in emergencies, 13

Henry, Prince (son of James I), 108, 162

Henry VI (Shakespeare), 118–19

Henry VII, King, 162, 223

Henry VIII, King, 25, 129–30, 162, 178, 204, 213, 234

High Court of Chancery, 94

Hogarth, William, 85–86, 144–45

Hospitals, 13

Hotels, 6–8, 9

House of Commons, 33, 91, 220, 222, 223, 226–30, 239

House of Lords, 209, 226–27

Hunt, Leigh, 208–10

Importance of Being Earnest, The (Wilde), 190–91

Information, asking for, 12–13

Inigo Place, 48

Inner Temple, 77, 79, 108–23
  gardens of, 118–19
  history of, 108–10, 123–25

Inns of Court, 77–124. *See also* Barristers; Inner Temple; Lincoln's Inn; Middle Temple
  pubs at, 99–100, 122–23, 248

IRA, 220–21

Jack the Ripper, 45, 117–18

Jagger, Mick, 177, 206

James, Henry, 211

James I, King, 30, 160–62

James II, King, 36, 58, 80, 89, 114, 115, 168

James Street, 63

Jeffreys, George, 114–15
Jekyll, Sir Joseph, 85
Jermyn, Henry, Earl of St. Albans, 131
Jermyn Street, 9, 131–33, 138–43
Jewel Tower, 224–26
John, Augustus, 191–92
Jones, Inigo, 25, 48, 60, 79
Justice Walk, 211

King's Bench Walk, 115–17
King's Head and Eight Bells (pub), 206
King's Road, 177, 180–81
King Street, 50, 57–63

Lady, The (magazine), 47–48
Lamb and Flag (pub), 56–57
Lambeth Palace, 223–24
Lancaster House, 165
Langtry, Lillie, 40, 45
Language, 3–4, 15–17
Law Courts, 100–3
Lawrence, T. E., 192, 231–33
Lawrence Street, 210–11
Lewes, George, 199
Lincoln's Inn, 77, 87–102
  chapel of, 93
  courts at, 93–94, 101–2
  gardens of, 94–95
Lincoln's Inn Archway, 98
Lincoln's Inn Fields, 79–86, 116
  park in, 85–86
Lindsey, Robert Bertie, Earl of, 81
Lindsey House, 79–83
Link extinguishers, 32–33, 237
Livingstone, Ken, 224
Lobb's (bootmaker), 155–56
Lock's (hatter), 155, 156
London, City of
  history of, 23–24
  royals' ceremonial entry into, 104

Look Back in Anger (Osborne), 179
Lower Robert Street, 38–39

McCartney, Paul, 201
Maiden Lane, 44–47, 63
Mall, The, 165, 168–69
Mansfield, Lord Chief Justice, 84, 116–17
Maps, 17–18
Marquis of Anglesey, The (pub), 66
Martin Chuzzlewit (Dickens), 122
Mary, Queen of Scots, 86
Mary I, Queen, 205
Mary II, Queen, 80
Mary of Modena, Queen, 168
Mary of Teck, Queen, 157
Middlemarch (Eliot), 198–99
Middlesex Street, 9–10
Middle Temple, 77, 79, 108–23
  entrances to, 106–10
  fountain court at, 122
  Grand Christmasses at, 121–22
  hall of, 120–22
  history of, 108–10, 123–25
Middle Temple Lane, 119–20
Mill on the Floss, The (Eliot), 198–99
Molay, Jacques de, 123–25
Monmouth, James Scott, Duke of, 114
Moore, Henry, 224
More, Thomas, 178, 211–13
Morning Star, 12
Mortimer, John, 110
Music halls, 58–60
My Fair Lady, 61

Nash, John, 165–66
National Portrait Gallery, 209
Neal Street, 63
Neave, Airey, 220, 221

New and Lingwood (clothing), 142
New Row, 50–51
Newspapers, 12
New Square, 94–96
Newton, Isaac, 140
Nightingale, Florence, 47, 87, 170
North, Lord Frederick, 239–41

Old Bailey, 100
Old Church Street, 213
Old Hall, 88, 93–94
Old Queen Street, 237
Oliver Twist (Dickens), 39
Olivier, Laurence, 184
Orford, Edward Russell, Earl of, 58, 62
Orwell, George, 26, 50
Osborne, John, 179
Outdoor markets, 9–10, 60, 62–63
Oxford Street, 7, 9

Paine, Tom, 81
Pall Mall, 160–62, 163
Palmerston, Henry John Temple, Lord, 239
Pankhurst, Emmeline, 223
Paper Buildings, 118
Paradise Walk, 193
Parliament, 30, 31, 50, 163, 166
    House of Commons, 33, 91, 220, 222, 223, 226–30, 239
    House of Lords, 209, 226–27
Parliament Buildings, 87, 219, 220–30
Parr, Catherine, 204
Paxton and Whitfield (cheese), 138
Penhaligon's (perfumes), 66–67
Pepys, Samuel, 33–36, 60, 69, 80–81, 93, 108, 115, 144, 153, 193–94, 222

Perceval, Spencer, 81
"Petticoat Lane," 9–10
Philippe IV, King of France, 123–25
Physic Garden, 178, 194–96
Pickering Place, 159
Pillar boxes, 187–89
Pitt, William, 90–91, 144
Plague, 108, 115, 153
Portobello Road, 10
Powlett, Charles, Marquis of Winchester, 80
Private Eye (magazine), 12, 147, 201
Profumo, John, 147
Prostitutes, 58–60, 70, 117, 160
Public schools, 233–37
Pubs, 10–11, 56–57, 66, 99–100, 122–23, 136–38, 160, 206, 211, 248–49
Pygmalion (Shaw), 61

Quant, Mary, 177, 180–81
Queen Anne's Gate, 237–43
Queensberry, John Douglas, Marquess of, 190, 191

Real Ale, 11, 66, 211
Red Lion, The (pub, Crown Passage), 160
Red Lion, The (pub, Duke of York Street), 136–38
Restaurants, 8–9, 45–47, 63–65, 136, 246–47
Richards, Keith, 177, 198
Rights of Man, The (Paine), 81
Robert Street, 40
Rochester, Earl of, 56
Rock Garden, The (restaurant), 63
Rodin, Auguste, 223
Romans, 23, 220–21
Rose Street, 56–57
Rossetti, Dante Gabriel, 178–79, 201–2
Royal Avenue, 181–84

Royal College of Surgeons, 86–87

Royal Courts of Justice, 99–101

Royal Court Theatre, 179

Royal Hospital, 183–84

Royal Hospital Road, 196

Royal Opera House, 25, 65–66

Royal Society of Arts, 40

Rule's (restaurant), 45–47, 63

Rumpole of the Bailey (Mortimer), 110

Ruskin, John, 192

Russell, Edward, Earl of Orford, 58, 62

Russell, Lord William, 80

Russell Square, 7

Russell Street, 63–66

Rysbrack, Michael, 194

Sackville, Charles, Earl of Dorset, 80–81

St. Albans, Henry Jermyn, Earl of, 131

St. Clement Danes Church, 43

St James's Church, 131–36

St. James's (district), 129–70
  gentlemen's clubs in, 130–31, 143–48, 160
  pubs in, 136–38, 160, 249
  restaurants in, 136, 247
  shops in, 130, 138–42, 143, 155–58, 159–60

St. James's Palace, 129–30, 145, 162–70

St. James's Park, 243

St. James's Place, 150

St. James's Street, 129, 130–31, 143–60

St. Leonard's Terrace, 184–89

St. Margaret's Church, 222

St. Mary's-le-Strand Church, 42–43

St. Paul's Church, 60–61, 62

St. Paul's Covent Garden, 48–50

Sargent, John Singer, 178, 191

Savoir Vivre (club), 145–47

Scott, George Gilbert, 90

Scott, James, Duke of Monmouth, 114

Seven Stars (pub), 99

Seymour, Thomas, 204

Shakespeare, William, 118–19, 121

Shaw, George Bernard, 61

Sheridan, Richard Brinsley, 67

She Stoops to Conquer (Goldsmith), 111

Shops, 8, 9–10, 51, 66–67, 98, 104–6, 130, 138–42, 143, 155–58, 159–60, 177, 180–81, 249–50

Slang, 3–4, 17

Sloane Street, 179

Smith, Richard, 145–47

Smith Street, 189

Smith Terrace, 189

Snow wells, 153–55

Soane, John, 84

Soane Museum, 86

Solicitors, 78, 96–98

Somerset House, 42

Spencer House, 152–53

Spies, 50, 236

Star Yard, 102

Stoker, Bram, 185–87, 206

Storey's Gate, 237

Stowell, Thomas, 118

Strand, The, 24–25, 42–43, 102–5

Sun, 12

Sunday Times, 201

Swan Walk, 193–96

Tavistock Street, 67

Taxis, 5, 9

Telephones, 14

Templar knights, 79, 113, 123–25

Temple, Henry John, Lord Palmerston, 239

Temple Bar, 104

Temple Church, 113

Terriss, William, 44–45

Texas, Republic of, 130, 159

Thackeray, William Makepeace, 151

Thatcher, Margaret, 91, 177, 196, 220, 224, 227

Theatre Royal, 67–73

Thurloe, John, 93

Time Out (magazine), 11–12

Times, 12

Tipping, 9

Tite Street, 189–93

"Tom and Jerry" cartoons, 150–51

Tower of London, 36, 115, 123, 204, 205

Transportation, 5–6

Tube, 5, 6

Turnbull and Asser (men's shirts), 143

Tutton's (restaurant), 63–65

Twelfth Night (Shakespeare), 121

Underground, 5, 6

University College Hospital, 13

Upper Cheyne Row, 208–10

Vardy, John, 152–53

Victoria, Queen, 79, 104, 136, 151, 169, 170, 187, 199, 200

Victoria Embankment Gardens, 26–28

Victoria Tower, 223, 226

Villiers, Barbara, Duchess of Cleveland, 131, 153

Villiers, George, Duke of Buckingham, 29–31

Villiers Street, 26–28

Voting, 60–61, 228–30

Waller, Edmund, 153–55, 162

Walpole, Horace, 104, 142–43, 145–46

Wars of the Roses, 118–19

Watergate Walk, 28–31

Weingott's (tobacconist), 104–5

Wellington Street, 66–67

Westminster, 23, 24, 103, 219–43

Westminster Abbey, 222–223

Westminster Fire Office, 57–58

Westminster Hall, 221–22, 226

Westminster School, 230, 233–37

What's On (magazine), 11

Wheeler's (restaurant), 136

Whistler, James McNeill, 178, 192–93

Whitehall, Palace of, 129, 130, 166. *See also* Parliament

White's (men's club), 143–44

Wilde, Oscar, 178, 189–91, 193

Wildy's (legal bookshop), 98

William I, King, 43

William III, King, 36–80

William IV, King, 158, 165, 169, 170

Winchester, Charles Powlett, Marquis of, 80

Wine bars, 28–29, 66

Woffington, Peg, 239, 241–42

World War I, 91

World War II, 94, 133, 157, 211

Wren, Christopher, 43, 131, 133, 184, 234

Wright, Peter, 50

York, Frederick Augustus, Duke of, 158, 180

York House, 29, 30, 31

York Place, 39

York Watergate, 29, 31

Young's (brewery), 11, 66